MW00638679

THE DRUG ESSAYS

THE DRUG ESSAYS

ALEISTER CROWLEY'S REFLECTIONS ON HASHISH, COCAINE & ABSINTHE

by

ALEISTER CROWLEY

Mockingbird
Press

Cover, "Crowley Smoking," by Joshua Davis, Copyright © 2019 Mockingbird Press
Foreword, by Elizabeth Ledbetter, Copyright © 2019 Mockingbird Press
About the Author attributable to Wikipedia, 2019 under CC BY-SA 3.0

Publisher's Cataloging-In-Publication Data

Crowely, Aleister, author; with Ledbetter, Elizabeth, editor
The Drug Essays: Aleister Crowley's Reflections on Hashish, Cocaine & Absinthe / Aleister Crowley; with Elizabeth Ledbetter.

Paperback   ISBN-13: 978-1-946774-71-2
Hardback   ISBN-13: 978-1-946774-72-9
Ebook   ISBN-13: 978-1-946774-73-6

Library of Congress Control Number: 2019954399

1. Religious doctrines (General)—Other. 2. Occult sciences—Magic. 3. Body Mind Spirit—Occultism. 4. Self Help—Substance Abuse & Addiction. 5. Mysticism, Magic & Occult Interests. 6. Health, Illness & Addiction. 7. Magic, Alchemy & Hermetic Thought, I. Aleister Crowley. II. Elizabeth Ledbetter. III. Title: Subtitle

BL473-490/ BF1585-1623 / OCC016000 / SEL013000 / VXW / JBFN / QRYX2

Type Set in Century Schoolbook / **Franklin Gothic Demi**

Mockingbird Press, Augusta, GA

CONTENTS

CONTENTS—*continued*

FOREWORD

ALEISTER CROWLEY was a larger than life figure, and a man of many contradictions. He was a self-declared prophet, who founded his own religion and tried to summon spirits to his aid, but he was also the son of a lay-preacher, who brought him up in a strict, evangelical church. Crowley believed himself to be both a man of science and a mystic. In his Confessions, Crowley boasted of his innate mathematical gifts and of his scientific training. He also claimed that, among other things, he had been born with all the signs of the Buddha and that he was a reincarnation of Pope Alexander VI.

As an adult, Crowley never tried to hide his fascination with sex and drugs. This earned him a reputation which still survives. The tabloid press of Crowley's time called him the "wickedest man alive." His own mother referred to him as "the Beast." Even in our own day, the prevailing image of Crowley is one of debauchery and transgression, and Crowley's image is often resurrected by those who dabble in the dark occult.

It is easy to stereotype Crowley as a libertine and a pleasure-seeker, a sort of 20th century Marquis de Sade with a mystic mind. But Crowley's writing makes clear he was far more complex than he is commonly given credit for. This collection, which brings together Crowley's drug essays, reveals a man at once ambitious and painfully earnest, with a seemingly endless interest in testing his own limits and broadening his understanding of the world.

* * * * *

Aleister Crowley was born Edward Alexander Crowley in 1875 to a wealthy family in England's West Midlands. (He changed his name to Aleister as a young man.) Crowley's parents were independently wealthy, heirs to the fortune from a family brewing company. His father, who was trained as an engineer, retired before Aleister was born. His parents were very devout Christians, members of the

Plymouth Brethren, which emphasized a literal application of the Bible to everyday life.

Members of the church were held to a strict code of conduct—drinking, smoking, and gambling were frowned upon. The brethren were not permitted to socialize with people who did not belong to their church. They held themselves apart from worldly customs, including celebration of Christmas and Easter, since those celebrations were not mentioned in the Bible.

Aleister's father became a lay-preacher when Aleister was a young boy. The young Aleister adored his father, whom he described as warm-hearted and intelligent, a natural leader. Aleister wanted desperately to emulate him. When he was sent to his first school—an evangelical institute—Aleister worked hard to be as pious as any boy there. Writing about the experience later (in the third person) he said,

> "It is a little difficult to explain the boy's psychology at this period. It was probably determined by his admiration for his father, the big, strong, hearty leader of men, who swayed thousands by his eloquence. He sincerely wished to follow in those mighty footsteps and so strove to imitate the great man as best he might."

When Aleister was just 10, though, his beloved father died of tongue cancer. Young Aleister's life was turned upside down. He was left in the care of his mother, whom he described as "a brainless bigot of the most narrow, logical and inhuman type." She took him to live with her brother, a "narrow" follower of evangelical Christianity. Aleister began to rebel almost immediately. By the time he was 16, he internally rejected the teachings of the church and began to drink, smoke, and experiment with sex.

Gone were the days when he sought to follow in his father's "mighty footsteps" and become the most Christian lad in school. In his *Confessions*, he boasts about reaching a turning point while having relations with a girl on his mother's bed. He began writing poetry about his affairs and his passions. Soon he began dabbling in magic and the occult, practices which surely would have scandalized the Plymouth Brethren.

While he was at Cambridge, Crowley joined the Hermetic Order of the Golden Dawn, a more or less secret society dedicated to "arcane ritual" and magic. Yeats was another member of the group, although the Irish poet and Crowley took an intense dislike to one another (Yeats called Crowley a "madman," and Crowley wrote that Yeats was inferior to him as a poet.) During his years at Cambridge, Crowley produced reams of poetry, traveled extensively, and experimented with magic. He left Cambridge without graduating, but he formed useful connections there.

Crowley founded his own religion, Thelema, in 1904. The faith still exists and its members regard Crowley as a prophet. Thelemic philosophy can be summed up in the phrase, "Do what thou wilt shall be the whole of the law; love is the law, love under will." (Thelema is a transliteration of the Greek noun meaning "will.") It is a highly individualist philosophy encouraging every person to seek out and fulfill the purpose of their own will.

Crowley eventually established an Abbey of Thelema in Sicily. The Abbey quickly attracted attention because of what many saw as its debauched lifestyle. A British tabloid called Crowley the "wickedest man alive" after one of his followers died at the Abbey. The Italian government ordered Crowley out by 1923, but the occultist never abandoned his own religion. He spent the rest of his life promoting it. Crowley died in 1947.

* * * * *

The essays in this collection represent Aleister Crowley's ideas and meditations on drugs. Part One explores Crowley's experiences with hashish and its uses in mystical rituals. Part Two examines cocaine and looks at whether it should be regulated by law. Finally, Part Three delves into the sensuality of absinthe and its role in society. The essays are fascinating, both for what they reveal about Crowley's views on drugs, and for the way they tap into some of the occultist's chief preoccupations: the quest for transcendence and the marriage of science to mysticism.

By his own account, Crowley was interested in drugs because he wanted to return to what he called the "pure soul" of the universe. He presents himself as a scientist, studying drugs for their ability to expand human awareness. He believed that hashish, in particular, was an ideal tool for putting man in touch with a deeper truth and consciousness. "Hashish at least gives proof of a new order of consciousness, and (it seems to me) it is this *prima facie* case that mystics have always needed to make out, and never have made out," he wrote.

Hashish opened the door to mystical experiences, but Crowley insisted the drug was nothing but a tool—it was never to be used as an end. "I have no use for hashish save as a preliminary demonstration that there exists another world attainable – somehow," Crowley insisted.

Crowley takes a similar view of cocaine. Using cocaine causes intense joy, he wrote; just one snort can make a man feel that he is being transformed from a "grub" to a "butterfly." But like any drug, cocaine is just a tool which can help people break out of their terres-trial lives and catch glimpses of the divine: "The happiness of cocaine is not passive or placid as that of beasts; it is self-conscious. It tells man what he is, and what he might be; it offers him the semblance of divinity, only that he may know himself a worm."

The end-goal of drugs, in Crowley's view, is to expand man's hori-zons. Crowley presents himself as an experimenter, engaged in study-ing the possible uses of drugs. However, most modern readers will find it hard to swallow the idea of Crowley as a pure researcher.

Crowley is most confusing when he discusses drug addiction. He acknowledges that addiction does happen, but he sees addiction as an outgrowth of a weak personality, not necessarily a function of drug-taking. That's why Crowley argued fervently against making drugs illegal. When he wrote "Cocaine," American reformers were pushing for drugs to be outlawed. Crowley took them on directly, writing, "you cannot cure a drug fiend; you cannot make him a useful citizen. He never was a good citizen, or he would not have fallen into slavery." Instead of banning substances, Crowley argued, the government should work harder to instill a "moral education" in its people, by teaching the values of self-control and good manners.

This kind of moralizing may surprise readers who associate Crow-ley with satanic rituals and the eating of excrement. The truth is, Crowley's writing often does not match the reality of his life. In fact, Crowley—who boasted that he was impervious to addiction—became completely addicted to both cocaine and heroin. He eventually agreed to let a doctor supervise his rehabilitation, but biographers believe that Crowley never really recovered. At best, he may have been liber-ated from its grip for a while, but he seems to have returned, again and again.

Why was Crowley so hesitant to write about drug addiction? There seems to be something at work here beyond the shame which is so often associated with dependence. Crowley had a deep need to portray himself as being above emotion and human weakness. This was a fundamental part of how he saw himself. In his Confessions, Crowley traced this characteristic lack of emotion back to earliest childhood. When he was a very small boy, his infant sister died. His parents took him to see her body, and, as he explains in the third person, he was unmoved:

> "The incident made a curious impression on him. He did not see why he should be disturbed so uselessly. He couldn't do any good; the child was dead; it was none of his business. This attitude continued through his life."

Crowley's notion of himself as a scientist, a man of cold logic and orderly methodology, was fundamental to his sense of self. His religion, Thelema, was built around the free expression of one's will. Considering this, it's no surprise that he left his addiction out of his drug essays.

Does the fact that Crowley ignored his own addiction impact the way we read his drug essays? Each reader will have to decide that for themselves. It would certainly be a mistake to take these essays entirely at face value, as the purely scientific and objective texts which Crowley intended them to be. But that, of course, doesn't mean that they lack literary value.

After all, Crowley the "pure scientist" had another side to him—one which thirsted for transcendence. This is why he wrote poetry instead of working out mathematical proofs. It's why he became a mountain climber and, it seems, why he experimented with drugs, sex, and perversions.

Crowley wrote that intoxication—whether from wine, drugs, or art—was what made it possible for man to rise above his "grub" life and achieve transcendence. He said it well here:

> "The surplus of Will must find issue in the elevation of the individual towards the Godhead; and the method of such elevation is by religion, love, and art. These three things are indissolubly bound up with wine, for they are species of intoxication."

Those lines come from Crowley's essay about absinthe, which is by far the most rhapsodic in this collection. Crowley makes no bones about his adoration for the liquor. He gets downright poetic about the drink's "opalescent" appearance and about the "rapture" it provokes. "Absinthe" is perceived as pure beauty, liberation from the grayness of the day-to-day.

Perhaps that's the gift that these essays can give us. Perhaps, rather than examining them too closely for truth and accuracy, it would be wise to read the essays in this book as objects of beauty. They are not cold, hard, facts. They are ideas, as opalescent as the absinthe in Crowley's glass. They read best when we can set aside our doubts and give ourselves up to the enjoyment of what this eccentric man was able to produce.

-   Elizabeth Ledbetter

PART I

THE PSYCHOLOGY OF HASHISH

CHAPTER 1

"The girders of the soul, which give her breathing, are easy to be unloosed... Nature teaches us, and the oracles also affirm, that even the evil germs of matter may alike become useful and good."
— ZOROASTER.

COMPARABLE to the Alf Laylah wa Laylah itself, a very Tower of Babel, partaking alike of truth both gross and subtle inextricably interwoven with the most fantastic fable, is our view of the Herb — Hashish — the Herb Dangerous. Of the investigators who have pierced even for a moment the magic veil of its glamour ecstatic many have been appalled, many disappointed. Few have dared to crush in arms of steel this burning daughter of the Jinn; to ravish from her poisonous scarlet lips the kisses of death, to force her serpent-smooth and serpent-stinging body down to some infernal torture-couch, and strike her into spasm as the lightning splits the cloud-wrack, only to read in her infinite sea-green eyes the awful price of her virginity — black madness.

Even supreme Richard Burton, who solved nigh every other riddle of the Eastern Sphinx, passed this one by. He took the drug for months "with no other symptom than increased appetite," and in his general attitude to hashish-intoxication (spoken of often in the "Nights") shows that he regards it as no more than a vice, and seems not to suspect that, vice or no, it had strange fruits; if not of the Tree of Life, at least of that other Tree, double and sinister and deadly . . . .

Nay! for I am of the Serpent's party: Knowledge is good, be the price what it may.

Such little fruit, then, as I may have culled from her autumnal breast (mere unripe berries, I confess!) I hasten to offer to my friends.

And lest the austerity of such a goddess be profaned by the least vestige of adornment I make haste to divest myself of whatever gold or jewelry of speech I may possess, to advance, my left breast bare, without timidity or rashness, into her temple, my hoped reward the lamb's skin of a clean heart, the badge of simple truthfulness and the apron of Innocence.

In order to keep this paper within limits, I may premise that the preparation and properties of *Cannabis indica* can be studied in the proper pharmaceutical treatises, though, as this drug is more potent psychologically than physically, all strictly medical account of it, so far as I am aware, have been hitherto both meagre and misleading. Deeper and clearer is the information to be gained from the brilliant studies by Baudelaire, unsurpassed for insight and impartiality, and Ludlow, tainted by admiration of de Quincey and the sentimentalists.[1]

My contribution to the subject will therefore be strictly personal, and so far incomplete; indeed in a sense valueless, since in such a matter personality may so largely outweigh all other factors of the problem. At the same time I must insist that my armour is more complete in several directions than that of my predecessors, inasmuch as I possess the advantage not only of a prolonged psychological training, a solid constitution, a temperament on which hashish acts by exciting perception (*Sañña*), quite unalloyed by sensation (*Vedana*) and a perfect scepticism; but also of more than an acquaintance with ceremonial drunkenness among many nations and with the magical or mystical processes of all times and all races. It may fairly be retorted upon me that this unique qualification of mine is the very factor which most vitiates my results. However . . .

With the question of intoxication considered as a key to knowledge let me begin, for from that side did I myself first suspect the existence of the drug which (as I now believe) is some sublimated or purified preparation of *Cannabis indica*.

---

[1] At the time of writing this article, I had only glanced rapidly through Baudelaire's essay. When I made the experiments, I knew only Ludlow, and the brief note in "Martindale and Westcott." My research results, therefore, such as they are, are unbiased by knowledge. The coincidences with Baudelaire now appear very striking.

CHAPTER 2

"Labour thou around the Strophalos of Hecate."

— ZOROASTER.

IN 1898-1899 I had just left Cambridge and was living in rooms in Chancery Lane, honoured by the presence of Allan Bennett (now Bhikkhu Ananda Metteyya) as my guest.

Together for many months we studied and practised Ceremonial Magic, and ransacked the ancient books and MSS. of the reputed sages for a key to the great mysteries of life and death. Not even fiction was neglected, and it was from fiction that we gathered one tiny seed-fact, which (in all these years) has germinated to the present essay.

Through the ages we found this one constant story. Stripped of its local and chronological accidents, it usually came to this — the writer would tell of a young man, a seeker after the Hidden Wisdom, who, in one circumstance or another, meets an adept; who, after sundry ordeals, obtains from the said adept, for good or ill, a certain mysterious drug or potion, with the result (at least) of opening the gate of the Other-world. This potion was identified with the *Elixir Vitæ* of the physical Alchemists, or one of their "Tinctures," most likely the "White Tincture" which transforms the base metal (normal perception of life) to silver (poetic conception), and we sought it by fruitless attempts to poison ourselves with every drug in (and out of) the Pharmacopoeia.

Like Huckleberry Finn's prayer, nuffin' come of it.

I must now, like the Baker, skip forty years, or rather eight, and reach a point where my travels in India had familiarised me with their systems of meditation and with the fact that many of the lesser Yogis employed hashish (whether vainly or no we shall discuss later) to obtain Samadhi, that oneness with the Universe, or with the Nothingness, which is the feeble expression by which alone we can shadow that supreme trance.

I had also the advantage of falling across Ludlow's book, and was struck by the circumstance that he, obviously ignorant of Vedantist and Yogic doctrines, yet approximately expressed them, though in a degraded and distorted form.

I was also aware of the prime agony of meditation, the dryness[2] (as Molinos calls it) which hardens and sterilises the soul.

The very practice which should flood it with light leads only to a darkness more terrible than death, a despair and disgust which only too often lead to abandonment, when in truth they should encourage, for that — as the oracles affirm — it is darkest before the dawn.

Meditation therefore annoyed me, as tightening and constricting the soul. I began to ask myself if the "dryness" was an essential part of the process. If by some means I could shake its catafalque of Mind, might not the Infinite Divine Spirit leap unfettered to the Light?

Who shall roll away the stone?

Let it not be imagined that I devised these thoughts from pure sloth or weariness. But with the mystical means then at my disposal, I required a period of days or of weeks to obtain any Result, such as Samadhi in one of its greater or lesser forms; and in England the difficulties were hardly to be overcome. I found it impossible to meditate in the cold, and fires will not last equably. Gas stinks abominably; heating apparatus does not heat; electricity has hitherto not been available. When I build my temple, I shall try it.

The food difficulty could be overcome by Messrs. Fortnum and Mason, the noise difficulty by training, the leisure difficulty by sending all business to the devil, the solitude difficulty by borrowing a vacant flat; but the British climate beat me. I hope one day to be rich enough to build a little house expressly for the purpose; but at present there is on the horizon no cloud even so large as the littlest finger of a man!

If only, therefore, I could reduce the necessary period to a few hours!

Moreover, I could persuade other people that mysticism was not all folly without insisting on their devoting a lifetime to studying under me; and if only I could convince a few competent observers — in such a matter I distrust even myself — Science would be bound to follow and to investigate, clear up the matter once for all, and, as I believed, and believe, arm itself with a new weapon ten thousand times more potent than the balance and the microscope.

Imagine me, therefore, if you please, selecting these few facts from the millions of others in the armoury of my brain, dovetailing them, and at last formulating an hypothesis verifiable by experiment.

---

[2] The period of the rule of Apophis in the mystic regenerative process Isis Apophis Osiris = I A O; or the Black Dragon in the alchemical translation from the First Matter of the Work into the Elixir.

CHAPTER 3

"But I evolve all these mysteries in the profound abyss of Mind."
— ZOROASTER.

THIS was my hypothesis:

"Perhaps hashish is the drug which 'loosens the girders of the soul,' but is in itself neither good nor bad. Perhaps, as Baudelaire thinks, it merely exaggerates and distorts the natural man and his mood of the moment." The whole of Ludlow's wonderful introspection seemed to me to fortify this suggestion.

"Well, then, let me see whether by first exalting myself mystically and continuing my invocations while the drug dissolved the matrix of the diamond soul, that diamond might not manifest limpid and sparkling, a radiance 'not of the Sun, nor of the Moon, nor of the Stars';" and then, of course, I remembered that this ceremonial intoxication constitutes the supreme ritual of all religions.

First, however, it was necessary to determine the normal action of the drug upon my particular organisation. There are various preparations of *Cannabis indica*, all alike in this, that their action is so uncertain as to be not easily or surely standardised. It is not even a question of reasonable limits: of two samples apparently alike one may be fifty times stronger than the other. A sample may apparently degenerate 50 per cent. in strength within a few days. Some samples may be totally inert. This fact has led to the almost total abandonment of the use of the drug in medicine.

Further, the personal equation counts for much. Allan Bennett in Chancery Lane had on one occasion taken sufficient Conium (hemlock) to kill forty men without the smallest result of any kind.

In Kandy I had (for the first time in my life) taken two hundred and twenty-five drops of Laudanum in five hours, also with no more result than would have been produced by ten drops upon the average man.

Our equation was therefore composed exclusively of variables, and wide variables at that! Nothing for it, then, but rule-of-thumb! The old Chancery Lane rule: begin with half the minimum dose of the Pharmacopoeia, and if nothing happens within the expected time, double the dose. If you go on long enough, something is nearly sure to happen!

CHAPTER 4

"The Mind of the Father said, Into Three! and immediately all things were so divided."

— ZOROASTER.

LET my readers be good enough to remember, then, that what follows concerns myself only. This must excuse the use of the first person, highly improper in a scientific essay, were it not that the personality of the experimenter is perhaps an essential. I cannot assert that my results would be achieved by another. Yet I have the strong conviction that I have eliminated many sources of error, and that my observations may possess a more absolute value in psychology than those of Ludlow or even of my great master Baudelaire. The few on whom I have been able to test the drug have in large measure confirmed, and in no way contradicted, my results.

In the first place, I make an absolute distinction between three effects of hashish, which may be, and I think probably are — so distinct they appear — due to three separate substances.

Possibly a simple stimulus-curve may account for it, but I do not think so.

1. The volatile aromatic effect (A).

This, the first evanescent symptom, gives the "thrill" described by Ludlow, as of a new pulse of power pervading one. Psychologically, the result is that one is thrown into an absolutely perfect state of introspection. One perceives one's thoughts and nothing but one's thoughts, and it is as thoughts that one perceives them. Material objects are only perceived as thoughts; in other words, in this respect, one possesses the direct consciousness of Berkeleyan idealism. The Ego and the Will are not involved; there is introspection of an almost if not quite purely impersonal type; that, and nothing more.

I am not to be understood as asserting that the results of this introspection are psychologically valid.

2. The toxic hallucinative effect (B).

With a sufficiently large dose — for it is possible to get effect (**A**) only as a transient phenomenon — the images of thought pass more rapidly through the brain, at last vertiginously fast. They are no longer recognized as thoughts, but imagined as exterior. The Will and the Ego become alarmed, and may be attacked and overwhelmed. This constitutes the main horror of the drug; it is to be combated by a highly — may I say magically? — trained will.

I trust my readers will concede that the practice of ceremonial magic and meditation, all occult theories apart, do lead the mind to immense power over its own imaginations.

The fear of being swept away in the tide of relentless images is a terrible experience. Woe to who yields!

3. The narcotic effect (C).

One simply goes off to sleep. This is not necessarily due to the brain-fatigue induced by (**A**) and (**B**); for with one sample of *Cannabis*, I found it to occur independently.

CHAPTER 5

"For this Paternal Intellect, which comprehendeth the Intelligibles and adorneth things ineffable, hath sowed symbols through the World... Comprehending that Intelligible with extended Mind; for the Intelligible is the flower of Mind... A similar fire flashingly extending through the rushings of air, or a Fire formless whence cometh the Image of a Voice, or even a flashing Light abounding, revolving, whirling forth, crying aloud. Also there is the vision of the fire-flashing Courser of Light, or also a Child, borne aloft on the shoulders of the Celestial Steed, fiery, or clothed with gold, or naked, or shooting with the bow shafts of Light and standing on the shoulders of the horse; then if thy meditation prolongeth itself, thou shalt unite all these symbols into the Form of a Lion."

— ZOROASTER.

THE most important of the psychological results of my experiments seem to me to lie in (**A**). I devoted much pains to obtaining this effect alone by taking only the minutest doses, by preparing myself physically and mentally for the experiment, and by seeking in every possible way to intensify and prolong the effect.

Simple impressions in normal consciousness are resolved by hashish into a concatenation of hieroglyphs of a purely symbolic type.

Just as we represent a horse by the five letters h-o-r-s-e, none of which has in itself the smallest relation to a horse, so an even simpler concept such as the letter A seems resolved into a set of pictures, a fairly large number, possibly a constant number, of them. These glyphs are perceived together, just as the skilled reader reads h-o-r-s-e as a single word, not letter by letter. These pictorial glyphs, letters as it were of the word which we call a thought, seem to stand at a definite distance in space behind the thought, the thought being farther from the perceiving soul. Looking at each glyph, one perceives, too, that itself is made up of other glyphs yet nearer to the Self, these glyphs, however, being formless and nameless; they are not truly perceived, but one is somehow aware of them.

Unfortunately, the tendency to fall into effect (**B**) makes it very

difficult to concentrate on the analysis of these ideas, so that one is
hurried on to a similar examination of the next thought. It is curious,
though, to notice how this analysis corresponds to the worlds of the
Qabalah, the single "pure soul" at the back of all, the shadowy "creative" world, the varied "formative world," and the single though con-
crete "material" world.

It puzzles one, too (at the time, in the very course of the analysis),
to ask: If the external simple impression be made up of so many
glyphs, and each of these again of many more, how can one ever return to the "pure soul"? For all the while one is clearly conscious of a
simple Ego or "pure soul" which perceives all this.

The only solution appears to lie in a metaphysical identification of
Monotheism and Pantheism.

Again, one is conscious of a double direction in the phenomena.
Not only is it true to say that the thoughts are analysed into glyphs
and so on, back to the pure soul; but also that the pure soul sends
forth the glyphs, which formulate the thought. Here again we must
identify the Atman system of Hinduism centered in Ego with the
Anatta system of Buddhism, in which the impressions are all.

Further, there arises an exceedingly remarkable state of mind, described in the *Bhagavad-Gita* (I quote Arnold):

"I, who am all, and made it all, abide its separate Lord."

The experience could not be better phrased. Zoroaster, too:

"Who first sprang from Mind, clothing the one Fire with the other
Fire, binding them together, that he might mingle the fountainous
craters, while preserving unsullied the brilliance of His own Fire."

"Containing all things in the one summit of his Hyparxis, He Himself subsists wholly beyond."

It is almost impossible to describe so purely metaphysical a state,
which involves clearly enough a contradiction in terms. Yet the consciousness is so vivid, so intense, so certain, that logic is condemned
unflinchingly as puerile.

The best escape for the logician is to argue that the three asser-
tions are closely consecutive, so closely that mind thinks them one;
just as the two points of a pair of compasses pressed upon certain
parts of the body are felt as one point only. While the mystic will mut-
ter some esoteric darkness about the true interpretation of the doctrine of the Trinity.

I think one should add that these results of my introspection are
almost certainly due to my own training in philosophy and magic,
and that nothing but the intensification of the introspective faculty is
due to the hashish. Probably, too, this effect (**A**) would be suppressed
or unnoticed in a subject who had never developed his introspection
at all.

Yet I am inclined to believe that this effect (**A**) is the true effect; and that Ludlow's "access of self-consciousness" is but the same operating on the organization of a man evidently nervous and timid.

CHAPTER 6

"The Intelligible is the principle of all section... The Mind of the Father whirled forth in re-echoing roar, comprehending by invincible Will Ideas omniform; which flying forth from that one fountain issued; for from the Father alike was the Will and the End (by which are they connected with the Father according to alternating life, though varying vehicles). But they were divided asunder, being by Intellectual Fire distributed into other Intellectuals. For the King of all previously placed before the polymorphous World a Type, intellectual, incorruptible, the imprint of whose form is sent forth through the World, by which the Universe shone forth decked with Ideas all-various, of which the foundation is One, One and alone. From this the others rush forth distributed and separated through the various bodies of the Universe, and are borne in swarms through its vast abysses, ever whirling forth in illimitable radiation... They are intellectual conceptions from the Paternal Fountain partaking abundantly of the brilliance of Fire in the culmination of unresting time... But the primary self-perfect Fountain of the Father poured forth these primogenial Ideas... The Soul, being a brilliant Fire, by the power of the Father remaineth immortal, and is Mistress of Life, and filleth up the many recesses of the bosom of the world."

— ZOROASTER.

THE alleged annihilation of time and space, which so frequently reappears in articles on hashish, seems to me solved more simply by a more accurate analysis of the phenomenon. The normal explanation involves the assumption that man naturally possesses a perfect and infallible "time-sense" as regular as a clock. Which is absurd; were it so, we should not need watches.

We are accustomed to work (whether the idea be philosophically tenable or not is not german to the matter) with a minimum cogitable both of space and of time. Just as a definite number of beats of the pendulum makes an hour, so mentally a less definite but far from indefinite number of thoughts makes an hour's consciousness. Perhaps powerful and vivid thoughts count for a longer lapse of time than weak ones. Deep sleep passes like an invisible electric discharge.

The apparently contrary fact that time seems short when we have been reading an interesting book or performing a pleasant and absorbing task is explained thus; the multitude of impressions is harmonised into one impression. Read an unharmonious and dull book, or an essay like this, and the time appears ineffably long.

The other contrary fact, that a minute's Samadhi appears as an eternity, though Samadhi is a single thought, is explained by the intensity of that thought and by other considerations which I shall hope to discuss more fully in section xiii. of this essay.

This, then, is what happens to the eater of hashish. For each impression he has thousands of glyphs (effect (**A**)) or in the more common[3] effect (**B**) the images are so multiplied and superimposed that all harmony is lost; the brain fails to keep pace with its impressions, still less to codify and control them. It finds then that from the idea *cat* to the idea *mouse* is a journey through the million dying echoes of cat to the million dawn-rays of mouse, and that the journey takes a million times as long as usual. This analysis of a thought into its dawn, noon, and sunset, is well drawn in Buddhist psychology.[4]

Often, too, most often, one of the "cat-echoes" will be so loud that the whole chain is shattered; the cat-echo becomes the dominant, and its harmonics (or inharmonics) themselves usurp the throne — and so on and so on — through countless ages of insane hallucination.

The same criticism applies to space; for in practice we judge of space by the time required to pass through it, either by the small angular or focussing movements of the eye or by our general experience. So that if I cross a room, and think a million thoughts on the way, the room seems immense. It is by the tedium of the journey, not by any hallucination of the physical eye, that this illusion is produced.

In writing my notes on one occasion I found that my right arm (which of course is not in the line of vision at all, normally) was many thousands of miles in extent. It was strange and difficult to control such colossal sweeps through space to the fine work of the pen. Yet my handwriting was no worse than usual — I admit this says little! It was the time that it apparently took to get one word written that caused the illusion of extravagant size, itself therefore a rational illusion, turned to phantastic absurdity by the excited imagination, which visualized it.

---

[3] More common, judging by the reports of Ludlow and others. I never permitted myself to fall under its dominion.
[4] See Mrs. Rhys David's book.

CHAPTER 7

"God is never so turned away from man, and never so much sendeth him new paths, as when he maketh ascent to divine speculations or works in a confused or disordered manner, and as it adds, with unhallowed lips, or unwashed feet. For of those who are thus negligent, the progress is imperfect, the impulses are vain, and the paths are dark."
— ZOROASTER.

ANOTHER and highly important result of thought-analysis is the criticism of thought as it arises. Just as the impressions are represented by pictorial glyphs, so each reflection upon an impression is accompanied by either one or two (more only when the control is imperfect) *critical* glyphs, as it were in small type, an annotation of approval or otherwise. Thus, a chain of thought A-B-C will have three approving pictures in a fainter key; the soul justifying the sequence. Should one continue A-B-C-E an opposing glyph will warn of the falsity, or at least cast doubt upon it. In the generally unstable condition of the thought, such a critical glyph may be strong enough to become the dominant; and then the whole line of thought breaks down. Let me give an example:

—Thought—	—Criticisms and Their Glyphs—
1. Man.	a man reaping — meaning "Good — go on."
	a horse = "True — Mill's definition."
2. Featherless Biped.	three horses in a field = "Are there no other featherless bipeds?"
	a stream = "Stop — Stop — Stop."
3. Was it Mill?	a tombstone on a hill = "Was it Locke?"
4. Locke? Locke?	a battle
	thousands of other violent glyphs

The whole mind is now a raging sea of confused thought: doubts, attempts to remember accurately who on earth first said "featherless biped," even an agony to recover thought 1, and start again. This one unfortunate weakness of thought 2 has drawn the thought-current away from the consideration of "man" to an academic question; and, as hashish goes, one is unlikely ever to get back to it. On the contrary, one of the critical glyphs attacking the thought "Locke? Locke?" will probably be strong enough to carry away the thought into a new channel, in its turn to be diverted. This at the best: for one is now ready to fall into the Maelstrom of effect (**B**).

There is only one remedy for this state of affairs, the discipline of thought which we call in its highest forms meditation and magic. The existence of the disease, it will be noticed, indeed perfectly explains the nature of thought-wandering as observed by me in simple meditation without drugs. It should be taken, I think, as the normal action of the untrained mind. So long as the thoughts are strongly thrown out, rational, the critical glyphs approve, and the thought-current moves harmoniously to its end. Such are the trained thought-currents of educated man. The irresponsible and aimless chatter of women and clergymen is the result of weak thoughts constantly drowned by their associated critical glyphs. Mere sympathetic glyphs, too, may be excited in really feeble intelligences. Puns and other false associations of thought are symptomatic of this imbecility. An extreme case is the classical "Cat-mousetrap-kittens" chain of the lunatic, when somebody said "hat."

As I said, there is but one remedy; we are all more or less subject to this wandering of thought, and we may all wisely seek to overcome it; that remedy is to train the mind constantly by severe methods; the logic of mathematics, the concentrated observation necessary in all branches of science, the still more elaborate and austere training of magic and meditation.

Too many people mistake reverie for meditation; the chemist's boy who thought Epsom salts was oxalic acid is a less dangerous person. Reverie is turning thought out to grass; meditation is putting him between the shafts.

The so-called poet with his vague dreams and ideals is indeed no better than a harmless lunatic; the true poet is the worker, who grips life's throat and wrings out its secret, who selects austerely and composes concisely, whose work is as true and clean as razor-steel, albeit its sweep is vaster and swifter than the sun's!

The discursive prattle of such superficial twaddlers as Longfellow and Tennyson is the most deadly poison of the mind. All this is true enough in the merest exoteric necessity of adult civilisation. But if we are to go further into the nature of things, to dive deeper than the chemist, soar higher than the poet, look wider than the astronomer, we must furnish ourselves with a blade of still better temper.

CHAPTER 8

*"It is not proper to understand that Intelligible One with vehe-
mence, but with the extended flame of far-reaching Mind, measuring
all things except that Intelligible. But it is requisite to understand this;
for if thou inclinest thy Mind thou wilt understand it, not earnestly;
but it is becoming to bring with thee a pure and inquiring sense, to
extend the void mind of thy soul to that Intelligible, that thou mayest
learn the Intelligible, because it subsisteth beyond Mind... Thou wilt
not understand it, as when understanding some common thing."*
— ZOROASTER.

IN other of my philosophical writings I have endeavored to show
that the ratiocinative faculty was in its nature unable to solve any
single problem of the universe.

Its *reductio ad absurdum* is clear enough in the gorgeous first section of Herbert Spencer's *First Principles*. Kant demonstrated the
Dualism and inherent Self-contradiction well enough in the *Prole-
gomena* and its four theses and their antitheses (§ 51); and Hegel's
Logic, if properly understood, would have brought the whole thing
into contempt.

But unfortunately the "common sense" of mankind retorted that after all the interior angles of every triangle *are* together equal to two
right-angles; and that a mental process which deduced this so accurately from a few simple axioms and definitions must be trustworthy;
adding something uncomplimentary about Germans and Metaphysics.

Both are right, and both are wrong. In the world of common sense,
reason works; in the world of philosophy, it doesn't. The metaphysical
deadlock is a real and not a verbal one. The inner nature of things is
not rational, at least so long as we are asked to define "rational" as
"rationalistic." Why should it be? Why should the rules of golf govern
the mechanics of the flight of a golf-ball?

It is this fact that has made it possible for the faith-mongers to
make head against the stream of philosophy. Fichte is really and
truly just as right and as wrong as Schelling; Hume is quite as im-
pregnable as Berkeley.

Let us not try to shirk the truth of it, either by the "common-sense" folly, or the "faith" folly, or the Hegelian folly.

It may, I think, be readily conceded that the reasoning faculty is not apodeictally absolute. It represents a stage in human thought, no more.

You cannot convince a savage of the truth of the Binomial Theorem; should we then be surprised if a mystic fails to convert a philosopher?

Yet he must try.

CHAPTER 9

"For being furnished with every kind of armour, and armed, he is similar to the goddess."

— ZOROASTER.

MY dear Professor, how can you expect me to believe this nonsense about bacteria?

Come, saith he, to the microscope; and behold them!

I don't see anything.

Just shift the fine adjustment — that screw there — to and fro very slowly!

I can't see —

Keep the left eye open; you'll see better!

Ah! — But how do I know? ...

Oh, there are a thousand questions to ask!

Is it fair observation to use lenses, which admittedly refract light and distort vision?

How do I know those specks are not dust?

Couldn't those things be in the air?

And so on.

The Professor can convince me, of course, and the more skeptical I am the more thoroughly I shall be convinced in the end; but not until I have learned to use a microscope. And when I have learned — a matter of some months, maybe years — how can I convince the next skeptic?

Only in the same way, by teaching him to use the instrument.

And suppose he retorts, "You have deliberately trained yourself to hallucination!" What answer have I? None that I know of. Save that microscopy has revolutionised surgery, &c., just as mysticism has revolutionised, again and again, the philosophies of mankind.

The analogy is a perfect one. By meditation we obtain the vision of a new world, even as the world of microorganisms was unsuspected for centuries of thinking — thinking without method — bricks without straw! Just so, also, the masters of meditation have erred. They have attained the Mystic Vision, written long books about it, assumed that the conclusions drawn from their vision were true on other planes — as if a microscopist were to stand for Parliament on the platform "Votes for Microbes"— never noted possible sources of error, fallen foul of sense and science, dropped into oblivion and deserved contempt.

I want to combine the methods, to check the old empirical mysticism by the precision of modern science.

Hashish at least gives proof of a new order of consciousness, and (it seems to me) it is this *primâ facie* case that mystics have always needed to make out, and never have made out.

But today I claim the hashish-phenomena as mental phenomena of the first importance; and I demand investigation.

I assert — more or less *ex cathedrâ* — that meditation will revolutionise our conception of the universe, just as the microscope has done.

Then my friend the physiologist remarks:

"But if you disturb the observing faculty with drugs and a special mental training, your results will be invalid."

And I reply:

"But if you disturb the observing faculty with lenses and a special mental training, your results will be invalid."

And he smiles gently:

"Patient experiment will prove to you that the microscope is reliable."

And I smile gently:

"Patient experiment will prove to you that meditation is reliable."

So there we are.

CHAPTER 10

"Stay not on the precipice with the dross of matter, for there is a place for thine image in a realm ever splendid... When thou seest a terrestrial demon approaching, cry aloud and sacrifice the stone Mnizourin."

— ZOROASTER.

As a boy at school I enjoyed a reputation for unparalleled cowardice; in the world I am equally accused of foolhardiness. The judgment of the boys was the better. The truth is that I have always been excessively cautious, have never willingly undertaken even the smallest risk.

The paradoxical result is that I have walked hundreds of miles unroped over snow-covered glaciers, and that nobody (so far as I know) has ever attempted to repeat my major climbs on Beachy Head. One may add a little grimly that the same remark applies to my excursions into the regions of the mind, the conscience, and the soul.

This is a bombastic prelude to a simple note on the precautions which I took in my experiments.

First, the use of the minutest care in estimating doses.

Secondly, the rule never to repeat my experiment before the lapse of at least a month.

Frankly, I doubt if these were necessary. I do not suppose my will to be abnormally strong; I believe rather that there is a definite type of drug-slave, born from his mother's womb; and that those who achieve it or have it thrust upon them are a very small percentage. In saying this I include such obsessions as music, religion, gambling, among drugs. Is the "Keswick week" less of a debauch than the navvy's Bank Holiday? There are people who rush from meeting to meeting, and give up their whole lives to this unwholesome excess of stimulant; they are happy nowhere else; they become as irritable as the cocaine-fiend, and render wretched the lives of those who are forced to come in contact with them.

Personally, I have never felt the bearing-rein of habit, though I have tried all the mental and physical poisons in turn. I smoke tobacco, the strongest tobacco, to excess, as I am told; yet a dozen times I have abandoned it, in order to see whether it had any hold upon me. It had none; I resigned it as cheerfully as a small boy resigns the tempting second half of his first cigar. After a meal (for the first day or two) my hands would go to my pockets from habit; finding nothing there, I would remember, laugh, and forget the subject at once.

I think, therefore, that we may dismiss the alleged danger of acquiring the hashish habit as fantastic.

Nobody will acquire the habit but the destined drug-slave; and he may just as well have the hashish habit as any other; he is sure to fall under the power of some enchantress.

All these alarmist reports, however, are really worthless, worthless at the best as the *omne ignotum pro terribili* fear of the savage for an unfamiliar shape of bottle, worthless at the worst as the temperance crank's account of the fatal effects of alcohol, the vegetarian's account of the dangers of meat-eating, or the missionary's account of the religion of the people he lives among.

The alleged sensuality of hashish — even Baudelaire admits it — simply does not exist for me, perhaps because there is no germ of lasciviousness in my mind. Of course if you excite, by whatever stimulus, a foul imagination, you will get pestilent effects.

When Queen Mab tickles the lawyer, he dreams of fees. So the people who associate nudity with debauchery, and see Piccadilly Circus in Monna Lisa, will probably obtain the fullest itching from the use of the drug.

I recommend it to them for, slaves and swine as they are, it must inevitably drag them to death by the road of a certifiable insanity less dangerous to society than their present subtler moral beastliness.

I think, too, that Baudelaire altogether exaggerates the reaction. I never felt the slightest fatigue or lassitude; but went from the experiments to my other work with accustomed freshness and energy. Probably, however, these effects depend largely on the sample of the drug employed; some may contain more active or grosser toxic agents than others.

Putting aside all these optimistic considerations, one is yet perfectly in accord with Baudelaire's conclusion, and for the same reason. (We discard his preliminary sophisms.)

I have no use for hashish save as a preliminary demonstration that there exists another world attainable — somehow. Possibly if pharmacists were to concentrate their efforts upon producing a standard drug, upon isolating the substance responsible for effect (**A**), and so on, we might find a reliable and harmless adjuvant to the process which I have optimistically named Scientific Illuminism.

But at least for the present we have not arrived so far. In my own case I should know fairly well what to do, well enough to get my little "loosening of the girders of the soul" at a guess twice in five times, perhaps more.

Not surely enough to guarantee results to other people without a lengthy series of experiments, still less to recommend them to try for themselves, unless under skilled supervision.

My present appeal is to recognised physiologists and psychologists to increase the number and accuracy of their researches on the introspective lines which I have laid down above, possibly with further aid from the pharmacist.

Once the pure physio-psychological action is determined, I shall then ask their further attention to the special results of combining the drug with the mystic process — always invoking trained observation — and from that moment the future of Scientific Illuminism will be assured.

I must add a paragraph or two on the nature of the mystic process and the general character of the transcendental states of consciousness resulting from its successful practice.

CHAPTER 11

"He maketh the whole World of Fire, Air, Water, and Earth, and of the all-nourishing Ether."

— Zoroaster.

ONE truth, says Browning, leads right to the world's end; and so I find it impossible to open a subject, however small in appearance, without discovering an universe. So, as I set myself to discuss the character of mystic states, it is immediately evident that if I am to render myself at all intelligible to English readers, a totally new system of classification must be thought out.

The classical Eight Jhanas will be useless to us; the Hindu system is almost as bad; the Qabalistic requires a preliminary knowledge of the Tree of Life whose explanation would require a volume to itself; but fortunately we have, in the Buddhist Skandhas and the Three Characteristics which deny them, a scheme easily assimilable to Western psychology.

In "Science and Buddhism" I dealt in some detail with these Skandhas; but I will briefly recapitulate.

In examining any phenomenon and analysing it we first notice its Name and Form (Nama and Rupa). "Here is a Rose," we say. In such a world live the entirely vulgar.

Next (with Berkeley) we perceive that this statement is false. There is an optical sensation (Vedana) of red; an olfactory sensation of fragrance; and so on. Even its weight, its space, are modifications of sense; and the whole statement is transformed into "Here is a pleasurable set of sensations which we group under the name of a rose." In such a world lives the sensuous artist.

Next, these modifications of sense are found to be but percepts; the pleasure or pain vanishes; and the sensations are observed coldly and clearly without allowing the mind to be affected. This perception (Sañña) is the world of the surgeon or the man of science.

Next, the perception itself is seen to be dependent on the nature of the observer, and his tendency (Sankhara) to perceive. The oyster gets no fun out of the rose. This state establishes a dualistic conception, such as Mansel was unable to transcend, and at the same time places the original rose in its cosmic place. The creative forces that have made the rose and the observer what they are, and established their relation to one another, are now the sole consciousness. Here lives the philosopher.

Easily enough, this state passes into one of pure consciousness (Viññanam). The rose and the observer and their tendencies and relations have somehow vanished. The phenomenon (not the original phenomenon, "a rose," but the phenomenon of the tendency to perceive the sensation of a rose) becomes a cloudless light; a static, no longer a dynamic conception. One has somehow got behind the veil of the universe. Here live the mystic and the true artist.

The Buddhist, however, does not stop here, for he alleges that even this consciousness is false; that like all things it has the Three Characteristics of Sorrow, Change, and Unsubstantiality.

Now all this analysis is a purely intellectual one, though perhaps it may be admitted that few philosophers have been capable of so profound and acute a resolution of phenomena. It has nothing to do with mysticism as such, but its rational truth makes it a suitable basis for our proposed classification of the mystic states which result from the many religious and magical methods in use among men.

CHAPTER 12

"The Vast sun, and the brilliant moon... O Ether, sun, and spirit of the moon! Ye, ye are the leaders of air! ...The Principles, which have understood the Intelligible works of the Father, He hath clothed in sensible works and bodies, being intermediate links existing to connect the Father with Matter, rendering apparent the Images of unapparent Natures, and inscribing the Unapparent in the Apparent frame of the World... There are certain Irrational Demons (mindless elementals), which derive their subsistence from the Aerial Rulers; wherfore the Oracle saith, Being the Charioteer of the Aerial, Terrestrial and Aquatic Dogs... The Aquatic when applied to Divine Natures signifies a Government inseparable from Water, and hence the Oracle calls the Aquatic Gods, Water Walkers... There are certain Water Elementals whom Orpheus calls Nereides, dwelling in the more elevated exhalations of Water, such as appear in damp, cloudy Air, whose bodies are sometimes seen (as Zoroaster taught) by more acute eyes, especially in Persia and Africa... Let the immortal depth of your soul lead you, but earnestly raise your eyes upwards."

— ZOROASTER.

NAMA-RUPA. — Purely material, and therefore shadowy and meaningless, are the innumerable shapes which haunt the mind of man. In one sense we must here include all purely sensory phenomena, and the images which memory presents to the mind which is endeavoring to concentrate itself upon a single thought.

In other systems of mysticism we must include all astral phantoms, divine or demoniac, which are merely seen or heard without further reflection upon them. To obtain these it is sufficient to perform the following experiment:

Sit down comfortably; it is perhaps best to begin in the dark.

Imagine as strongly as possible your own figure standing in front of you.

Transfer your consciousness to that figure, so that you look down upon your physical body in the chair. (This is usually the one difficulty.)

Feeling perfectly at home in your imagined body, let that body rise
through the air to a great height.

Stop. Look around you. Probably the eyes of your "astral" body will
be closed. It is sometimes difficult to open them.

You will then perceive all sorts of forms, varying as you travel
about. Their nature will depend almost entirely on your power of control. Some people may even perceive the phantoms of delirium and
madness, and truly go mad from fear and horror.

Let the "astral" body return and sit down, coinciding with the
physical body.

Closely unite the two: the experiment is over.

Practice makes perfect.

This practice is delusive and even dangerous; it is best to precede
and follow it by a carefully performed "Lesser Ritual of the Penta-
gram."[5] Better still, have a skilled teacher. The experiment is an easy
one; with two pupils only (of some dozens) I have failed, and that
completely; with the others the first experiment was a success.

We must include, too, in this section the forms appearing in answer to the rites of ceremonial magic.

(Consult "Goetia," the "Key of Solomon," Eliphaz Levi, Cornelius
Agrippa, Pietro di Abano, Barrett and others for instructions.)

These forms are more solid and real, much more dangerous, and
are excessively difficult to obtain. I have known very few successful
practitioners.

All these forms and names are almost infinitely varied. The grosser
visual and auditory phenomena of hashish belong to the group. It is
not just to suppose that a vision of a Divine being of ineffable splen-
dour is necessarily of higher type than this shadowy form-world. Mistake on this point has led many a student astray. Highest among
these things are the three visual and seven auditory phenomena of
Yoga. (We omit consideration of the other senses; the subject requires
a volume.)

These are referred to the Sun, the Moon, and Fire; and their appearance marks the attainment of Dhyana. They are dazzling, and
accompanied with such intense though passionless bliss that they par-
take of the nature of Vedana and may under certain conditions even
rise to touch Sañntilde. Of the auditory are sounds heard like bells,
elephants, thunder, trumpets, sea-shells, "the sweet-souled Vina," and
so on; they are of less importance and are much more common.

As one would expect, such forms leave little impress upon the
memory. Yet they are seductive enough, and I am afraid that the very

---

[5] Mr. Haddo's suggestions have been officially taken up and a book of careful
instruction compiled. See Liber O. — ED.

great majority of mystics live all their lives wandering about in this vain world of shadows and of shells.

All this, too, is the pleasant aspect of the affair. Here belong the awful shapes of delirium and madness, which obsess and destroy the soul that fails to control and dismiss them. Here lives the Dweller of the Threshold, that concentration into a single symbol of the Despair and Terror of the Universe and of the Self. Yet on all the paths is He, ready to smite whoso falters or swerves, though he have attained almost the last height.

How many have I known, like Childe Roland and his peers, who have come to that Dark Tower! One young, one brave, one pure — lost! lost! penned in the hells of matter, swept away in the whirling waters of insane vision, true victims of the hashish of the soul.

What poignant agony, what moaning abjectness, what self-disgust! What vain folly (of all true hope forlorn!) to seek in drugs, in drink, in the pistol or the cord, the paradise they have forfeited by a moment's weakness or a moment's wavering!

This "two-handed engine at the door stands ready to smite" each one of us who has not attained to Arahatship, admission to the Great White Brotherhood. Is it not enough to make us throw away our atheism and exclaim, "O God be merciful to me a sinner, and keep me in the way of Truth!" Nay, for those of us who know what triple silver cord of moonlight binds the red blood of our heart to the Ineffable Crown of Brilliance, who have seen what Angel stands in the moonray, who have known the perfume and the vision, seen the drops of dew supernal stand on the silver lamen of the forehead — for us is neither fear nor pride, but silence in the one thought of the One beyond all thought.

The world of phantoms has no terror left; we can take the blood of the Black Dragon for our Red Tincture. We understand the precept *Visita Interiora Terrae Rectificando Invenias Occultum Lapidem;* and harnessing to our triumphal car the White Eagle and the Green Lion we voyage at our ease upon the Path of the Chameleon, by the Towers of Iron and the Fountains of Supernal Dew, unto that black unutterable Sea most still.

CHAPTER 13

"From the Cavities of the Earth leap forth the terrestrial dog-faced demons, showing no true sign unto mortal man... Go not forth when the Lictor passeth by... Direct not thy mind to the vast surfaces of the Earth; for the Plant of Truth grows not upon the ground. Nor measure the motions of the Sun, collecting rules, for he is carried by the Eternal Will of the Father, and not for your sake alone. Dismiss (from your mind) the impetuous course of the Moon, for she moveth always by the power of necessity. The progression of the Stars was not generated for your sake. The wide aerial flight of birds gives not true knowledge, nor the dissection of the entrails of victims; they are all mere toys, the basis of mercenary fraud; flee from these if you would enter the sacred paradise of piety, where Virtue, Wisdom, and Equity are assembled... Stoop not down unto the darkly splendid World; wherein continually lieth a faithless Depth, and Hades wrapped in clouds, delighting in unintelligible images, precipitous, winding, a black ever-rolling Abyss; ever espousing a Body unluminous, formless and void... Stoop not down, for a precipice lieth beneath the Earth, reached by a descending Ladder which hath Seven Steps, and therein is established the Throne of an evil and fatal force... Stay not on the Precipice with the dross of Matter, for there is a place for thy Image in a realm ever splendid... Invoke not the visible Image of the Soul of Nature... Look not upon Nature, for her name is fatal... It becometh you not to behold them before your body is initiated, since by always alluring they seduce the souls from the sacred mysteries... Bring her not forth, lest in departing she retain something... The Light-hating World, and the winding currents by which many are drawn down."

— ZOROASTER.

IT may be useful here to distinguish once and for all between false and real mystical phenomena; for in the previous section we have spoken of both without distinction. In the "astral visions" the consciousness is hardly disturbed; in magical evocations it is intensely exalted; but it is still bound by its original conditions. The Ego is still opposed to the non-Ego; time is, if altered in rate, still there; so, too, is

Space the sort of Space we are all conscious of. Again, the phenomena observed follow the usual laws of growth and decay.

But all true mystical phenomena contradict these conditions.

In the first place, the Ego and non-Ego unite explosively, their product having none of the qualities of either. It is precisely such a phenomenon as the direct combination of Hydrogen and Chlorine. The first thing observed is the flash; in our analogy, the ecstasy of Ananda (bliss) attending the Dhyana. And as this flash does not aid us to analyse the Hydrochloric acid gas, so the Ananda prevents us by startling us from perceiving the true nature of the phenomenon. In higher mystic states, then, we find that the Yogi or Magician has learnt how to suppress it.

But the combination of the elements will usually be a definite single act of catastrophic energy. This act, too, does not take place in time or space as we know them. I think that for the first time of experiencing a Dhyana it is necessarily single. Certain mystical methods may teach us to retain the image; but the criterion of true Dhyana is the singleness, so totally opposed as it is to the vague and varying phantoms of the "astral plane."

The new consciousness resulting from the combination is, too, always a simple one. Even where it is infinitely complex, as in Atmadarshana or the Vision of the Universal Peacock, its oneness is the truer of these two contradictory truths.

So for the matter of time and space. All time is filled; all space is filled; the phenomenon is infinite and eternal.

This is true even though its singleness makes the duration of the phenomenon but one minimum cogitabile. In short, it is experienced in some other kind of time, some other kind of space.

There is nothing irrational about this. Non-Euclidean geometries, for example, are possible, and may be true. It is only necessary to a theory of the universe that it should be true to itself within itself; for there is no other thing outside by which we can check our calculations. Nor is it inconceivable that many of these worlds may exist, interpenetrating. Assume four dimensions, and there is room for an infinite number of them. For though a plane fills a square completely, it must always leave a cube entirely empty.

Concerning the laws which govern this new realm we can say nothing here. The most mystics have been led away from the proper line of research, usually by the baser (i.e., the emotional or devotional) attractions of the Vedana-phenomena which we are about to notice; but perhaps even the best must be baffled by the non-congruity of their Experience with the symbols of language.

One may add that the language difficulty is in some ways an essential one. Language begins with simple expression of the common needs of the most animal life. Hence we see that all sciences have formulated a technical language of their own, not to be understood of the common people. The reproach against mystics that their symbols are obscure is just as well founded as a similar reproach against the algebraist or the chemist. A paper at the Chemical Society is often completely intelligible only to some three or four of the odd hundred distinguished chemists in the room.

What is gained to "popular science" is lost to exactitude; and in a paper of this sort I fear rather the reproach of my mystical masers than that of the bewildered crowd.

More important and certain than the mere characteristics of mystic traces in themselves is the great and vital diagnostic that the result of a true trance is to inspire the Yogi with power to do first-rate work in his own department.

People who produce maudlin and hysterical gush, inane sentimentality, who are faddists, fools, drivellers, dodderers — these I refuse to accept as mystics. The true phenomena of mysticism can only occur in a high-class brain and a healthy brain; and their action on that brain is to repose it, to fortify it, to make it more capable of lofty and continuous thought. Beware of the sheep in lions' skins, the asses that bray and think "the tiger roars!"

Physically too the mystic is to be known by his atmosphere of power, cleanliness and light; by his self-control, his concentration of thought and action, his vigour, his patience.

You will rarely find them at afternoon tea gossiping about clairvoyance, or even "playing Adam."

What? you don't know how to play "Adam"? And you call yourself a sage? Tut!

The game of "Adam" is played as follows.

Take a key, a Bible, an elastic band.

Open the Bible at random till you find a favourable text.

There insert the key, leaving the barrel and ring outside.

Put the elastic band round the book, so as to fix the key firmly in it.

Balance the whole arrangement by putting your thumb and that of the Assistant Magus of Art under the ring, thumb against thumb.

(An important but, as I hold, heterodox school of adepts employ the forefinger.)

Keep very still; and ask your question: "Adam, Adam, tell me true! Shall I —" &c.

If the Bible turns in a dextro-rotary manner the answer is "yes"; if in the opposite direction, "no."

This sublime method of tearing out the heart of destiny is evidently derived from a slightly more elaborate one in the "Key of Solomon" (Book I., chap. ix.) for detecting theft, which is done with a sieve, and which I supposed (until "Adam" advised me to the contrary) to represent the lowest debauchery in which the human intellect could wallow.

The game is, however, much esteemed by charlatan clairvoyants; and I can well understand their indignation at finding that I do not recognise their proficiency in this game and that of swindling and blackmail as entitling them to a seat at the Round Table of the Adepts.

Let us, however that may be, return to our classification.

CHAPTER 14

"There is a certain Intelligible One whom it becometh you to under-stand with the Flower of Mind... Having mingled the Vital Spark, from two according substances, Mind and Divine Spirit, as a third to these He added Holy Love, the venerable Charioteer uniting all things... Filling the Soul with profound Love... The Soul of man does in a manner clasp God to herself. Having nothing mortal, she is wholly inebriated with God. For she glorieth in the harmony under which the moral body subsisteth... As rays of Light his locks flow forth, ending in acute points."

— ZOROASTER.

VEDANA. — Pertaining to Sensation we may first notice in the be-ginner's concentrating mind the class of distracting thoughts which refer to the emotions. The taking of pleasure in, or the endurance of pain from, the meditation itself is in particular to be dreaded.

Of mystic phenomena we may notice the immense class of devo-tional apparitions. Vishnu, Christ, Jehovah and other deities appear in response to long-continued and passionate love. See *Bhagavad Gita,* chap. xi., the visions of many Catholic saints, Teresa, Gertrude, Francis and others, Anna Kingsford (*Clothed with the Sun,* Part III), Idra Rabba Qadisha and so on.

The Virgin Mary is a favourite with many; it is all one phenomenon.

Observe, though, that many such apparitions are not of the Dhyana type at all; they are mostly mere hallucinations of the "astral plane." In Chapter 11. we have indicated the diagnostics.

Methods of obtaining these states are to be found in any book on Bhakta Yoga — Swami Vivekananda's is the best I know of — and in Loyola's "Exercitios Espirituales," whose discipline and method is, in my opinion, unsurpassed.

These phenomena are nearly always tainted with sexuality, and are excessively dangerous from this cause. "Dirt is matter in the wrong place," and to mix, consciously or unconsciously, either morality or immorality with religion is dirty; and dirt makes disease. The victim becomes a fanatic at the best, at the worst and most frequent a driveller.

Of a lower type are the loves of Magi and invoked elementals. As Levi says, "the love of the Magus for such beings is insensate, and may destroy him." It surely will, if he beware not in time.

Higher again because more purely formless and for this reason truer to the Vedana type are the ecstasies of joy and agony experienced by such men as Luther, Fox, Molinos, and others. Professor William James treats most adequately of this matter in his *Varieties of Religious Experience*.

The limitations of this stage are first, its absorption in self; secondly, its almost always insuperable tendency to self-limitation and narrowness.

Two mystics, the one wallowing in Jesus and the other in Vishnu, will describe their experiences in almost identical language, yet denounce each other as "heathen" and "Mlechha" respectively.

Among hashish phenomena the correspondences are those of the intense emotions experienced (well described by de Quincey [opium] and Ludlow in particular). Such are fear, pride, love, laughter, anguish, and the rest.

In the case of Vishvarupadarshana (the vision of Vishnu) and even of such results as those of St. Francis and St. Ignatius, the best mystics may steer clear of the selfishness, narrowness, and emotionalism, and raise their experience to the type of Sañña or even of Sankhara.

The *Bhagavad Gita* certainly reaches the latter height — or at least a reflection from that height — at one or two points.

We must not omit to attribute to this section the lower aspect of what Abramelin the Mage calls the Knowledge and Conversation of the Holy Guardian Angel, another (and less metaphysically pretentious) way of speaking of the "Higher Self" or "Genius." It is indeed but a low aspect, for in truth the phenomenon pertains to Viññanam. Yet in simpler souls this peculiar Grace condescends — may one say? — to this level, just as a father may join in the games of his child, thus gaining its sympathy and confidence as a basis for a higher union.

CHAPTER 15

"The Mind of the Father riding on the subtle guiders which glitter with the inflexible tracings of relentless fire... The Oracles assert that the types of Characters and of other Divine visions appear in the Ether (or Astral Light)."

— ZOROASTER.

SAÑÑA.— Chief among the phenomena of Saññā, in the case of the beginner trying to concentrate his mind, are those disturbing thoughts which analyse the very process itself. Harder to destroy are they than the others, since they come no longer from memory or physical conditions, but from the practice itself, so that they cannot be shut off, but must needs be faced and conquered directly.

In the mystic world, we come to those strange metaphysical ecstasies which (I am convinced) lie behind many philosophical dogmas.

St. Athanasius had probably experienced something of this type when he penned his insane creed. So the Hindus with their attempts to affirm Parabrahma by denying him all qualities, their dogmas of the "pairs of opposites," their assertion of Sat-Chit-Ananda as transcending these pairs; so too perhaps with Herbert Spencer it was direct Samadhic perception of this Saññā type that led him to formulate his irrational doctrine of Transcendental Realism, just as (certainly) Berkeley's doctrine arose from Samadhi of the type of Vedana. For the stigma of this class of mystic experience is undoubtedly first its resolution of all concepts into purely formless and passionless perception, secondly (and above this), its transcendence of the laws of thought, as we have been accustomed to understand them.

(This is only in part true. Keynes' "Formal Logic," profoundly studied, leads one perilously close to the suprarational. The eminent professor is perhaps hardly aware of how his eagle-flights have brushed the sun with their fiery wings.)

If a dweller upon this plane meditate upon a God, his first experience of that God will be no longer of His appearance or of His effect upon himself, but rather of His nature in some region of pure thought. In the case of the god Osiris, for example, he will no longer express his vision by the name Osiris or by the green face, by the white robes starred with the three active colours, by the crown and by the crook and scourge; nor will he chant wondrous hymns of the descent into Amennti, the death and resurrection of the God; but he will express all this by some pure symbol, such as the cross, the hexagram, or even the number 6. And those upon his plane will understand him.

Here, too, we must class the revelations of the pure Qabalah, and the discovery of the relations between symbols.

So exalted in truth are the states upon this Sañña grade that the rational man will almost always fail to understand them. Of the Rupa visions he has some experience, if only in analogy; he calls the mystic of Rupa a silly fool; so too of Vedana, whose mystic he calls a besotted ass; but the mystic of Sañña appears to him as a raving lunatic.

The hashish correspondences of this stage are the mental analyses which I have gone into so fully above, sections v. and vii.

The methods for obtaining success in this matter are far more formidable than those previously sufficient. The whole mind must be intended for long unbroken periods, concentrated absolutely upon its own working until this becomes normal to it, when the state called Pratyahara is attained The first result will be its resolution into disconnected impressions.

Following this may occur a terrible experience; the consciousness of the disconnectedness of all phenomena, and of the units of consciousness of the observer. Both the Universe and the Self are insane. The mind may become a total blank, the only relief (strange as it sounds) being the all but intolerable mental agony of the consciousness. This agony, belonging to the lower stage of Vedana, is the drag, ever pulling back the mystic as he endeavours to break down the blackness of his insanity. Yet the unity of its anguish is the proof of its Selfhood, and the earnest of its resurrection from the abyss. Such a mystic state may last through several days, perhaps through weeks. I should not care to assert limitations. The slightest error in the process would almost certainly result in permanent and hopeless melancholia; suicide might be the most fortunate termination.

CHAPTER 16

"O how the world hath inflexible intellectual rulers!"

— ZOROASTER.

SANKHARA. — The reader will notice — I trust with pained sympathy — the increasing difficulty of expressing these results of meditation in language. At this point one almost desires to exclaim with Fichte that if it were only possible to start all over again, one would begin by inventing a totally new scheme of symbolism.

Here in Sankhara, hashish-analogy is somewhat at fault. Possibly the conviction of the irresistibility of the connection of cause and effect, the consciousness of the necessity of subject and object to each other through immutable glyphs may represent it. It may be that my experience of hashish is even more imperfect than I have supposed, and that more gifted experimenters might fill this gap.

In the beginner's concentration — though he is hardly to be called a beginner at this stage — Sankhara presents a terrible obstacle. For the distraction to his even flow of thought is that very flow itself; not as in Sañña, the accidents necessarily arising from that flow, as it were the rocks in the bed of the stream, but the law of gravitation itself, its necessary tendency to follow its own course. So that the good young Yogi finds himself thus awkwardly placed; that having created a mighty engine and removed all conceivable impediments to its smooth working, he is now confronted by the inertia of all that majesty and might.

Frankenstein!

The mystic states of Sankhara are more awful and tremendous than any we have yet noticed. Atmadarshana, for instance, is only to be described feebly (yet I fear unintelligibly, even so) by speaking of a consciousness of the entire Universe as One, and as All, in Its necessary relation to Itself in and out of Time and Space.

Here, too, is the result of Sammasati, a comprehension of one's own self and its relation to, and identity with, everything.

...But I feel that I am drivelling. The effort to think of these things, to translate them into the language of philosophy, gives the feeling —

I grope and find no other expression — that one's head is going to blow off. One feels inclined to get up and shout for very feebleness, and only the utter fatuity of that or or any other method of obtaining relief keeps one quietly writing. One feels, too, like the old woman in Theresa Raquin, dumb and paralysed even while bursting with the tremendous secret. Small wonder than if the adepts demand years of training before the things themselves are thought! "Look not upon the Visible Image of the Soul of Nature; for Her Name is Fatality; it becometh not thy body to behold Her, until it be first cleansed by the Sacred Mysteries."

The methods most practical and easy of obtaining these states are principally as follow:

First, the cultivation of the "magical memory." The practice is to remember the events of the day backwards; i.e., first dinner, then tea, lunch, and breakfast. Except, of course, that by this time one has abandoned meals for ever! The memory acquires the habit, and eventually goes on working backwards through sleep, back, back, through birth and previous states until (saith Bhikhu Ananda Metteyya) going ever back through the past one comes right round to the future — "Which is pretty, but I don't know what it means!"

I think it right to mention that I never obtained any sort of success in this meditation, and only give it on hearsay. The real key to the stage is Sammasati — Right Recollection. One considers all known factors which have gone to make one up such as one is, oneself and not another. Clearly the omission of a single minute item must alter the whole course of events. Consider then, why thus, and not thus.

"Explore the River of the Soul, whence, or in what order you have come: so that although you have become a servant to the body, you may again rise to the Order from which you descended, joining works to sacred reason."

Why was I born in England, not in Wales?

Why were my parents just who they were and not others?

Why did I take to climbing, not to cricket?

So for every known fact that concerns one — and all known facts concern one, if only to ask, "Why do I know this fact?"

How does it all fit in? It must, for the Universe is not insane — that blackness has been passed.

Who then am I? And why? And why?

Reaching ecstasy or Samadhi through this channel, the riddle of Kamma is answered, and one is able to enter the realm of pure consciousness. The Universe, mastered long ere now in its effects, is at last mastered in its causes; and it is indeed a Magister of the Temple who can say:

Vi Veri Vniversum Vivvs Vici.

CHAPTER 17

"All things subsist together in the Intelligible World."
—ZOROASTER.

I must insert a short note on the word Samadhi, source of infinite misunderstanding.

Etymologically it is composed of Sam (Greek [sigma upsilon nu]), together with, and Adhi (Heb. Adonai), the Lord, especially the Personal Lord, or Holy Guardian Angel.

The Hindus accordingly use it to name that state of mind in which subject and object, becoming One, have disappeared. Just as H combines with Cl, and HCl results, so the Yogi combines with the object of his meditation (perhaps his own heart) and these disappearing, Vishnu appears. It is not that the Yogi perceives Vishnu.[6]

The Yogi is gone, just as the Hydrogen is gone. It is not that the Heart has become Vishnu, or that Vishnu has filled the heart. The heart is gone, just as the Chlorine is gone. There is the tube, and it is full of HCl out of all relation to its elements, through the result of their union. (I purposely take the "elementary chemistry" view of the matter.)

Samadhi is therefore with the Hindu a result, the result of results indeed. There are higher and lower forms. That called Nirvikalpa-Samadhi, when the trance results from banishing thought altogether, instead of concentrating on one thought, is the highest kind.

But, with the Buddhist, Samadhi, though the state of mind meant is the same, is not an end, but a means.

The holy-man-of-the-East must keep this state of mind unimpaired during his whole life, using it as a weapon to attack the Three

---

[6] The difficulty of showing this makes the author of the Bhagavad Gita descend to Rupa-symbols when he ought to have been in Viññanam (chap. xi.). It is quite essential to change the subject of the sentence. Thus the Autobiography of a Mystic would run: foetus, babe, child, boy, youth, man, 418. There is no personal identity as a link between the man who is on the brink of "attainment" and the Being who arises in him, annihilating him, and Whom he subsequently remembers as his "Genius."

Characteristics (the anthithesis of Nibbana) even as one uses one's normal dualistic consciousness to attack that dualism.

But I must observe that this idea is so tremendous that I almost doubt its possibility, and tremble as to my own understanding of it. Samadhi twelve seconds in duration is a phenomenon to shake the soul of a man, to uproot his Kamma, to destroy his Identity — and Bhikku Ananda Metteyya cheerfully talks of practically perpetual Samadhi as the first step to attainment!

The Hindu, too, asks this question.

"I," he says, "define Phenomena as changeful and Atman the Noumenon as without change. When challenged, I merely retort by distinguishing between Atman and Paramatman. You say the same, but for Atman you say 'Nibbana.'"

The Buddhist can only retort, rudely enough: There is no Atman; and there is Nibbana.

The Hindu probably mutters something about criticism of Nibbana having forced some Buddhists to a conception of Parinibbana, simply but neatly defined as That to which none of the criticisms apply! Yet Atman and Nibbana are defined in almost identical terms.

It is clearly idle for us who know neither perfectly to attempt to arbitrate in so delicate an imbroglio. On the contrary, we had better set to and attain them both, and That which combines, denies, and transcends them both. Words are cheap!

CHAPTER 18

"In this the things without figure are figured... A similar Fire flashingly extending through the rushings of Air, or a Fire formless whence cometh the Image of a Voice, or even a flashing Light abounding, revolving, whirling forth, crying aloud. Also there is the vision of the fire-flashing Courser of Light, or also a Child, borne aloft on the shoulders of the Celestial Steed, fiery, or clothed with gold, or naked, or shooting with the bow shafts of Light, and standing on the shoulders of the horse; then if thy meditation prolongeth itself, thou shalt unite all these Symbols into the form of a Lion... But God is He having the Head of the Hawk."

— ZOROASTER.

VIÑÑANAM. — If hashish-analogy be able to assist us here, it is in that supreme state in which the man has built himself up into God. One may doubt whether the drug alone ever does this. It is perhaps only the destined adept who, momentarily freed by the dissolving action of the drug from the chain of the four lower Skandhas, obtains this knowledge which is his by right, totally inept as he may be to do so by any ordinary methods.

In the case of the aspirant to meditation, this stage is even more terrible than the last. He has, to use our previous figures, suspended the law of gravitation; the stream is still, and the Sun of the soul is faithfully reflected in its brilliance; the mighty engine is stopped.

But — there it is! We have got rid of motion, but matter remains. (Again must I apologise for taking so elementary a view of physics.) And while there is a particle of matter, it must fill the Universe — there is no place for spirit. His thought is controlled and smooth; his thought (even!) is stopped: but there the thought is. Immutable it abides, stronger than ever in its silence and vastness; and — O unhappy one! that which can be thought is not true.

Thou hast taken thee the lies, those little foxes that spoil the grapes. Lie after lie thou has suppressed; and what hast thou achieved?

Thou hast smitten all the illusions — O miserable slave! All thou hast done is to harmonise and weld all the lies and illusions into one universal lie, one infinite illusion. It is one; there is nothing to oppose to it. Thou art ten million-fold more in the grip of Maya than ever, thou who callest thyself Parabrahma, Hua, IAO!

The mystic states of this grade are the final and perfect identity of the Self with the Holy Guardian Angel, the Vision of Pan, the Four Formless States of Buddhism, namely, Samadhi upon consciousness, Space, Nothing, and that which is neither P nor p', in logical phraseology. Here, too, we should place Shivadarshana, the Vision of the Destruction of the Universe, the Opening of the Eye of Shiva.

(Which is why adepts of this stage wear an eye as a badge.)

Of this vision what can one say, save that the Universe, as previously known through Atmadarshana, is annihilated? Yet the negation of this phrase is only apparent; the sense is that all that negative Atmadarshana is destroyed; it is only an illusion that goes. Yet there is indeed Nothing in its place — and the only way to express the matter is to spell that Nothing with a capital N.

If the rationalist reader has had the quite super-Stylite patience to read to this point, he will surely now at last throw down the book with an ethically justifiable curse.

Yet I beg him to believe that there is a shade of difference between me and a paradox-monger. I am not playing with words — Lord knows how I wish I could! I find that they play with me! — I am honestly and soberly trying to set down that which I know, that which I know better than I know anything else in the world, that which so transcends and excels all other experience that I am all on fire to proclaim it.

Yet I fail utterly. I have given my life to the study of the English language; I am supposed by my flatterers to have some little facility of expression, especially, one may agree, in conveying the extremes of thought of all kinds. Yet here I want to burn down the Universe for lack of a language. So the angry mood passes, and one understands how one's predecessors, in the same predicament, got out of it by quietly painting a "Heart girt with a Serpent" or a "Winged Globe" or some similar device.

If I persist, seeing that my little gift of language must be mine for some purpose, and therefore for this purpose, since no other purpose can there be, let my rationalist friends excuse me, as the agony of my impotence most terribly avenges them.

Concerning the methods of obtaining these particular states, I am almost at one with Sri Parananda, my godly friend, when he talks of "the Grace of the Lord Shiva," and with my ungodly friend Bhikkhu Ananda Metteyya, when he hints that the accidental coincidence of the circumferences of the Nibbana-Dhatu and the Samsara-Chakra with the Brahmarandra of the sphere of the 99-year-old-Talipot-palm-like sucking Arahat may have something to do with it.

Plainly, we know so very little; so few ever attain this class of experience that one is perhaps hardly justified in maintaining (as I always have maintained and that stoutly) that the reward is according to the work. It may conceivably be that work does not affect the question, as it clearly does in the lower grades, it may be that an outsider may pull off the big thing — Agnosco!

Still, I advise people to work at it.

Perhaps the most direct method is that of sitting in your Ajna Chakra (that point in your brain where thoughts rise, a point to be discovered and rendered self-conscious by repeated experiment) and without thinking of anything whatever, killing the thoughts as they rise with a single smack, like a child killing flies. The difficulty is of course to kill them without thinking of the killing, which thought is naturally just as bad as any other thought. I never got any good out of this method myself. It may, I believe, happen with fair frequency that in the course of any advanced meditation or invocation this particular type of spiritual experience may suddenly arise without apparent cause.

Anyway, let us hope so!

As a matter of practical politics, I think that a judicious mixture of the methods of East and West is likely to give the best results.

Let the young Adept, for example, master thoroughly the groundwork of the Hindu system.

Let him master Asana, posture, so that he can sit motionless for hours without any message from his body reaching and so disturbing his brain. Let him include in his accomplishments Paranayama, control of the breath and of the vital nervous currents which react in sympathy with it.

Let him then exalt to the utmost his soul by the appropriate ritual of ceremonial magic; and when by this means he has most thoroughly identified himself with the Supreme, let him, as that Supreme One, continue to meditate with intense force upon Himself, until his sphere is entirely filled with the single Thought.

Lastly, if this, the male energy, suffice not, let him transform it into a pure and perfect emptiness and passivity, as of one waiting for the Beloved One, with intense longing rendered passionless by the certainty that He will come.

Then, it may be, the Eye will open upon him, and the tomb of his Pyramid be unsealed.

It is impossible in a few words to explain thoroughly this eclectic system; for each act and thought of the ritual demands an expert teacher, and even a good pupil might study for years before mastering the method. By which time he might not impossibly have discovered one of his own.

Howbeit, I must do my best; and if by that best I can help "the least of these little ones," so much the better.

CHAPTER 19

"The Intelligible subsisteth beyond Mind."

— ZOROASTER.

NERODHA-SAMAPATTI. — It must be very satisfactory, you will probably be thinking, to wear that Eye as a badge, to have got so near to the End.

And that is where the joke comes in. Yet to the adept the Anglo-Indian proverb, "A jok's a jok (leech) but a jok up your nose is no jok" (Nose is not the word; but no matter!), may occur with painful intensity.

For he is no nearer to Nibbana than when he started. Though he has stripped off all the husks of thought and touched Thought itself, even attaining to Negation of thought; yet he is still upon the plane of Thought. And — that which can be thought is not true.

All his righteousness is as filthy rags; even his eternity of Shivadarshana, his stored crores of Mahakalpas in the Arupa-Brahma-Lokas must pass; he must come back to his horses — and this time as a horse-fly.

So then he must abandon the whole series of ecstasies; all this time he has been on the wrong road. For the Three Characteristics are true of Viññanam as they are of Rupa; Change, Sorrow, Unsubstantiality.

He has only one asset; the habit of One-pointedness — Ekagrata. He may be all kinds of a black magician; but at least he has learnt to concentrate his mind. But what is he to aim at? Hashish-analogy is better than ever here; for Nibbana stands to the attainment of the Eight Jhanas, the Four Formless States [kappa.tau.lambda.] as the Decalogue does to any of his hashish-states. It has nothing whatever to do with it.

All this time he has been walking round the circumference of a wheel, cheerfully singing "Nearer, my God, to Thee; Nearer to Thee!" while his God is in the centre. He has done the medicine-man trick, and wasted a lot of maidens in the hope of making rain. So — one must suppose, for here I reach a point where, as Mr. Waite jeers, we are driven to take refuge in portentous darkness and irretrievable mystery (because we don't know anything about it) — he sits down and contemplates the Three Characteristics. This will presumably be very difficult to do because he is probably (for all the "Grace of the Lord Shiva" business) an expert in the Viññanam trances, and having thus created an eternal Universe and an even more eternal Absence of Universe, both of which, too, are probably mere masses of Sat - Chit - Ananda (Being - Knowledge - Bliss) while he is trying to think of Change - Sorrow - Unsubstantiality.

At last, as I imagine, probably without foundation, he succeeds in seeing first the truth and then the falsity of the Three Characteristics — and that is Nibbana.

(One may explain, as with Samadhi, that the man is not "in" Nibbana; the Characteristics are not "in" Nibbana: but — Nibbana is.)

It would be easy to string up a paradox-scheme in which Change, not-Change, both-Change-and-not-Change, and neither-Change-nor-not-Change were all four perceived at once; and indeed some authors have done something very like this; but, between you and me, I don't believe they knew anything about it; and as I certainly don't know anything myself, if it's all the same to you, I'd rather leave the subject alone. We really can't have another Hargrave Jennings on "The Rosicrucians: Their Rites and Mysteries."

So there the matter must rest. I have added this section for the sake of completeness; but it is all hearsay. I am too blind to see the necessity of the section at all; I am far from convinced that the Viññanam phenomena do not represent finality; so stupendous are they that even to one who is accustomed to them it must always be difficult to imagine a state not merely beyond them but out of their dimension. Yet? ... Perhaps that which I now urge is indeed the Great Illusion. ...

At least, having adopted the Buddhist Skandhas as the basis of my classification, I was bound in mere courtesy to give the Buddhist doctrine as I have heard it from the one man who really understands it, Bhikkhu Ananda Metteyya.

If I could only understand Him...!

CHAPTER 20

"If thou extendest the Firey Mind to the work of piety, thou wilt pre-serve the fluxible body... For three days and no longer need ye sacrifice."

— ZOROASTER.

WE are at the end of our little digression upon mystic states, and may cheerfully return to the consideration of Scientific Illuminism. We have had, you may say, a poor half-pennyworth of Science to an intolerable deal of Illuminism. Well, that is what I wanted you to say. Were it not so, I would not have spent these two nights over this paper, when I want to be fresh every morning to go to the Prado and gloat over Velasquez!

Here, gentlemen, are a number of genuine mystic states; some home-grown, some imported. Please tell us what they are! (You are fond of telling us what things are.) It is useless to label the whole lot as insane: nor are they unimportant. In my view, most of the great men of the world have known them; themselves attributed their greatness to these experiences, and I really do not see why admittedly lesser men should contradict them. I hope to argue this point at greater length when I am better documented; but at the very least, these states are of the most extraordinary interest. Even as insanities, they would demand the strictest investigation from the light they throw upon the working of the brain. But as it is! All the sacred literature of the world is full of them; all the art and poetry of all time is inspired by them; and, by the Lord Harry! we know nothing about them. Nothing but what vague and troubled reflections the minds of the mystics themselves, untrained in accuracy of observation, bring back from the fountains of light; nothing but what quacks exploit, and dotards drivel of.

Think of what we claim! That concentration and its results can open the Closed Palace of the King, and answer the Riddle of the Sphinx. All science only brings us up to a blind wall, the wall of Philosophy; here is your great Ram to batter a breach and let in the forlorn hope of the Children of the Curse to storm the heights of heaven.

One single trained observer with five years' work, less money than would build a bakehouse, and no more help than his dozen of volunteer students could give him, would earn himself a fame loftier than the stars, and set mankind on the royal road to the solution of the One great problem. Scientific Illuminism would have deserved its name, or mysticism would have received a blow which would save another young fool like myself from wasting his whole life on so senseless a study and enable him to engage in the nobler career of cheating and duping his fellows in the accredited spheres of commerce and politics, to say nothing of the grosser knaveries of the liberal professions.

But I have no doubts. Let the investigator study his own brain on the lines I have laid down, possibly in the first place with the aid of hashish or some better physical expedient, to overcome the dull scepticism which is begotten of idleness upon ignorance; it is useless to study the no-brain of another, on the strength of a reputation for fraud, as the spiritualist investigators seem to do. Your own brain is the best; next, the trained and vigorous brains of clever and educated men, in perfect health, honest and wary.

You will get more from them than you will from some maudlin hysteric professional mountebank. All talk to the contrary is the merest froth; Mohammed was a great lawgiver and a great fighter; try your experiment with the sane, and not with the crazy!

True, you will get hallucinations more easily with the unsound; but you will never, never, never find a woman or a degenerate who is capable of any trance of type higher than Vedana. Take my word for it!

No! take my word for nothing: try all things; hold fast that which is good!

MADRID,
August 1908, O.S.

PART II

COCAINE

CHAPTER 1

"There is a happy land, far, far, away."

— HYMN.

OF all the graces that cluster about the throne of Venus the most timid and elusive is that maiden whom mortals call Happiness. None is so eagerly pursued; none is so hard to win. Indeed, only the saints and martyrs, unknown usually to their fellow-men, have made her theirs; and they have attained her by burning out the Ego-sense in themselves with the white-hot steel of meditation, by dissolving themselves in that divine ocean of Consciousness whose foam is passionless and perfect bliss.

To others, Happiness only comes as by chance; when least sought, perhaps she is there. Seek, and ye shall not find; ask, and ye shall not receive; knock, and it shall not be opened unto you. Happiness is always a divine accident. It is not a definite quality; it is the bloom of circumstances. It is useless to mix its ingredients; the experiments in life which have produced it in the past may be repeated endlessly, and with infinite skill and variety — in vain.

It seems more than a fairy story that so metaphysical an entity should yet be producible in a moment by no means of wisdom, no formula of magic, but by a simple herb. The wisest man cannot add happiness to others, though they be dowered with youth, beauty, wealth, health, wit and love; the lowest blackguard shivering in rags, destitute, diseased, old, craven, stupid, a mere morass of envy, may have it with one swift-sucked breath. The thing is as paradoxical as life, as mystical as death.

Look at this shining heap of crystals! They are Hydrochloride of Cocaine. The geologist will think of mica; to me, the mountaineer, they are like those gleaming feathery flakes of snow, flowering mostly where rocks jut from the ice of crevassed glaciers that wind and sun have kissed to ghostliness. To those who know not the great hills, they may suggest the snow that spangles trees with blossoms glittering and lucid. The kingdom of faery has such jewels. To him who tastes them in his nostrils — to their acolyte and slave — they must seem as if the dew of the breath of some great demon of Immensity were frozen by the cold of space upon his beard.

For there was never any elixir so instant magic as cocaine. Give it to no matter whom, Choose me the last losel on the earth; let him suffer all the tortures of disease; take hope, take faith, take love away from him. Then look, see the back of that worn hand, its skin discolored and wrinkled, perhaps inflamed with agonizing eczema, perhaps putrid with some malignant sore, He places on it that shimmering snow, a few grains only, a little pile of starry dust. The wasted arm is slowly raised to the head that is little more than a skull; the feeble breath draws in that radiant powder. Now we must wait, One minute — perhaps five minutes.

Then happens the miracle of miracles, as sure as death, and yet as masterful as life; a thing more miraculous, because so sudden, so apart from the usual course of evolution. *Natura non facit saltum—* nature never makes a leap. True — therefore this miracle is a thing as it were against nature.

The melancholy vanishes; the eyes shine; the wan mouth smiles. Almost manly vigor returns, or seems to return. At least faith, hope and love throng very eagerly to the dance; all that was lost is found.

The man is happy.

To one the drug may bring liveliness, to another languor; to another creative force, to another tireless energy, to another glamour, and to yet another lust. But each in his way is happy. Think of it! — so simple and so transcendental! The man is happy!

I have traveled in every quarter of the globe; I have seen such wonders of Nature that my pen yet splutters when I try to tell them; I have seen many a miracle of the genius of man; but I have never seen a marvel like to this.

CHAPTER 2

IS there not a school of philosophers, cold and cynical, that accounts God to be a mocker? That thinks He takes His pleasure in contempt of the littleness of His creatures? They should base their theses on cocaine! For here is bitterness, irony, cruelty ineffable. This gift of sudden and sure happiness is given but to tantalize. The story of Job holds no such acrid draught. What were more icy hate, fiend comedy than this, to offer such a boon, and add "This you must not take?" Could not we be left to brave the miseries of life, bad as they are, without this master pang, to know perfection of all joy within our reach, and the price of that joy a tenfold quickening of our anguish?

The happiness of cocaine is not passive or placid as that of beasts; it is self-conscious. It tells man what he is, and what he might be; it offers him the semblance of divinity, only that he may know himself a worm. It awakes discontent so acutely that never shall it sleep again. It creates hunger. Give cocaine to a man already wise, schooled to the world, morally forceful, a man of intelligence and self-control. If he be really master of himself, it will do him no harm. He will know it for a snare: he will beware of repeating such experiments as he may make; and the glimpse of his goal may possibly even spur him to its attainment by those means which God has appointed for His saints.

But give it to the clod, to the self-indulgent, to the blasé — to the average man, in a word — and he is lost. He says, and his logic is perfect: This is what I want. He knows not, neither can know, the true path; and the false path is the only one for him. There is cocaine at his need, and he takes it again and again. The contrast between his grub life and his butterfly life is too bitter for his unphilosophic soul to bear; he refuses to take the brimstone with the treacle.

And so he can no longer tolerate the moments of unhappiness; that is, of normal life; for he now so names it. The intervals between his indulgences diminish.

And alas! the power of the drug diminishes with fearful pace. The doses wax; the pleasures wane. Side-issues, invisible at first, arise; they are like devils with flaming pitchforks in their hands. A single trial of the drug brings no noticeable reaction in a healthy man. He goes to bed in due season, sleeps well, and wakes fresh. South American Indians habitually chew this drug in its crude form, when upon the march, and accomplish prodigies, defying hunger, thirst, and fatigue, But they only use it in extremity; and long rest with ample food enables the body to rebuild its capital. Also, savages, unlike most dwellers in cities, have moral sense and force.

The same is true of the Chinese and Indians in their use of opium. Every one uses it, and only in the rarest cases does it become a vice. It is with them almost as tobacco is with us.

But to one who abuses cocaine for his pleasure nature soon speaks; and is not heard. The nerves weary of the constant stimulation; they need rest and food. There is a point at which the jaded horse no longer answers whip and spur. He stumbles, falls a quivering heap, gasps out his life.

So perishes the slave of cocaine. With every nerve clamoring, all he can do is to renew the lash of the poison. The pharmaceutical effect is over; the toxic effect accumulates. The nerves become insane. The victim begins to have hallucinations. "See! There is a grey cat in that chair. I said nothing, but it has been there all the time."

Or, there are rats. "I love to watch them running up the curtains. Oh yes! I know they are not real rats. That's a real rat, though, on the floor. I nearly killed it that time. That is the original rat I saw; it's a real rat. I saw it first on my window-sill one night."

Such, quietly enough spoken, is mania. And soon the pleasure passes; is followed by its opposite, as Eros by Anteros.

"Oh no! they never come near me." A few days pass, and they are crawling on the skin, gnawing interminably and intolerably, loathsome and remorseless.

It is needless to picture the end, prolonged as this may be, for despite the baffling skill developed by the drug-lust, the insane condition hampers the patient, and often forced abstinence for a while goes far to appease the physical and mental symptoms. Then a new supply is procured, and with tenfold zest the maniac, taking the bit between his teeth, gallops to the black edge of death.

And before that death come all the torments of damnation. The time-sense is destroyed, so that an hour's abstinence may hold more horrors than a century of normal time-and-space-bound pain.

Psychologists little understand how the physiological cycle of life, and the normality of the brain, make existence petty both for good and ill. To realize it, fast for a day or two; see how life drags with a constant subconscious ache. With drug hunger, this effect is multiplied a thousandfold. Time itself is abolished; the real metaphysical eternal hell is actually present in the consciousness which has lost its limits without finding Him who is without limit.

CHAPTER 3

MUCH of this is well known; the dramatic sense has forced me to emphasize what is commonly understood, because of the height of the tragedy — or of the comedy, if one have that power of detachment from mankind which we attribute only to the greatest of men, to the Aristophanes, the Shakespeares, the Balzacs, the Rabelais, the Voltaires, the Byrons, that power which makes poets at one time pitiful of the woes of men, at another gleefully contemptuous of their discomfitures.

But I should wiselier have emphasized the fact that the very best men may use this drug, and many another, with benefit to themselves and to humanity. Even as the Indians of whom I spoke above, they will use it only to accomplish some work which they could not do without it. I instance Herbert Spencer, who took morphine daily, never exceeding an appointed dose. Wilkie Collins, too, overcame the agony of rheumatic gout with laudanum, and gave us masterpieces not surpassed.

Some went too far. Baudelaire crucified himself, mind and body, in his love for humanity; Verlaine became at last the slave where he had been so long the master. Francis Thompson killed himself with opium; so did Edgar Allen Poe. James Thomson did the same with alcohol. The cases of de Quincey and H. G. Ludlow are lesser, but similar, with laudanum and hashish, respectively. The great Paracelsus, who discovered hydrogen, zinc and opium, deliberately employed the excitement of alcohol, counterbalanced by violent physical exercise, to bring out the powers of his mind.

Coleridge did his best while under opium, and we owe the loss of the end of Kubla Khan to the interruption of an importunate "man from Porlock," ever accursed in the history of the human race!

CHAPTER 4

CONSIDER the debt of mankind to opium. Is it acquitted by the deaths of a few wastrels from its abuse?

For the importance of this paper is the discussion of the practical question: should drugs be accessible to the public?

Here I pause in order to beg the indulgence of the American people. I am obliged to take a stand-point at once startling and unpopular. I am compelled to utter certain terrible truths. I am in the unenviable position of one who asks others to shut their eyes to the particular that they may thereby visualize the general.

But I believe that in the matter of legislation America is proceeding in the main upon a totally false theory. I believe that constructive morality is better than repression. I believe that democracy, more than any other form of government, should trust the people, as it specifically pretends to do.

Now it seems to me better and bolder tactics to attack the opposite theory at its very strongest point.

It should be shown that not even in the most arguable case is a government justified in restricting use on account of abuse; or allowing justification, let us dispute about expediency.

So, to the bastion — should "habit-forming" drugs be accessible to the public?

The matter is of immediate interest; for the admitted failure of the Harrison Law has brought about a new proposal — one to make bad worse.

I will not here argue the grand thesis of liberty. Free men have long since decided it. Who will maintain that Christ's willing sacrifice of his life was immoral, because it robbed the State of a useful taxpayer?

No; a man's life is his own, and he has the right to destroy it as he will, unless he too egregiously intrude on the privileges of his neighbours.

But this is just the point. In modern times the whole community is one's neighbor, and one must not damage that. Very good; then there are pros and cons, and a balance to be struck.

In America the prohibition idea in all things is carried, mostly by hysterical newspapers, to a fanatical extreme. "Sensation at any cost by Sunday next" is the equivalent in most editorial rooms of the alleged German order to capture Calais. Hence the dangers of anything and everything are celebrated dithyrambically by the Corybants of the press, and the only remedy is prohibition. A shoots B with a revolver; remedy, the Sullivan law. In practice, this works well enough; for the law is not enforced against the householder who keeps a revolver for his protection, but is a handy weapon against the gangster, and saves the police the trouble of proving felonious intent.

But it is the idea that was wrong. Recently a man shot his family and himself with a rifle fitted with a Maxim silencer. Remedy, a bill to prohibit Maxim silencer! No perception that, if the man had not had a weapon at all, he would have strangled his family with his hands.

American reformers seem to have no idea, at any time or in any connection, that the only remedy for wrong is right; that moral education, self-control, good manners, will save the world; and that legislation is not merely a broken reed, but a suffocating vapor. Further, an excess of legislation defeats its own ends. It makes the whole population criminals, and turns them all into policemen and police spies. The moral health of such a people is ruined for ever; only revolution can save it.

Now in America the Harrison law makes it theoretically impossible for the layman, difficult even for the physician, to obtain "narcotic drugs." But every other Chinese laundry is a distributing centre for cocaine, morphia, and heroin. Negroes and street peddlers also do a Toaring trade. Some people figure that one in every five persons in Manhattan is addicted to one or other of these drugs. I can hardly believe this estimate, though the craving for amusement is maniacal among this people who have so little care for art, literature, or music, who have, in short, none of the resources that the folk of other nations, in their own cultivated minds, possess.

CHAPTER 5

IT was a very weary person, that hot Summer afternoon in 1909, who tramped into Logroño. Even the river seemed too lazy to flow, and stood about in pools, with its tongue hanging out, so to speak. The air shimmered softly; in the town the terraces of the cafés were thronged with people. They had nothing to do, and a grim determination to do it. They were sipping the rough wine of the Pyrenees, or the Riojo of the South well watered, or toying with bocks of pale beer. If any of them could have read Major-General O'Ryan's address to the American soldier, they would have supposed his mind to be affected.

"Alcohol, whether you call it beer, wine, whisky, or by any other name, is a breeder of inefficiency. While it affects men differently, the results are the same, in that all affected by it cease for the time to be normal. Some become forgetful, others quarrelsome. Some become noisy, some get sick, some get sleepy, others have their passions greatly stimulated."

As for ourselves, we were on the march to Madrid. We were obliged to hurry. A week, or a month, or a year at most, and we must leave Logroño in obedience to the trumpet call of duty.

However, we determined to forget it, for the time. We sat down, and exchanged views and experiences with the natives. From the fact that we were hurrying, they adjudged us to be anarchists, and were rather relieved at our explanation that we were "mad Englishmen." And we were all happy together; and I am still kicking myself for a fool that I ever went on to Madrid.

If one is at a dinner party in London or New York, one is plunged into an abyss of dullness. There is no subject of general interest; there is no wit; it is like waiting for a train. In London one overcomes one´s environment by drinking a bottle of champagne as quickly as possible; in New York one piles in cocktails. The light wines and beers of Europe, taken in moderate measure, are no good; there is not time to be happy, so one must be excited instead. Dining alone, or with friends, as opposed to a party, one can be quite at ease with Burgundy or Bordeaux. One has all night to be happy, and one does not have to speed. But the regular New Yorker has not time even for a dinner-party! He almost regrets the hour when his office closes. His brain is still busy with his plans. When he wants "pleasure," he calculates that he can spare just half an hour for it. He has to pour the strongest liquors down his throat at the greatest possible rate.

Now imagine this man — or this woman — with time available slightly curtailed. He can no longer waste ten minutes in obtaining "pleasure"; or he dare not drink openly on account of other people. Well, his remedy is simple; he can get immediate action out of cocaine. There is no smell; he can be as secret as any elder of the church can wish.

The mischief of civilization is the intensive life, which demands intensive stimulation. Human nature requires pleasure; wholesome pleasures require leisure; we must choose between intoxication and the siesta. There are no cocaine fiends in Logroño,

Moreover, in the absence of a Climate, life demands a Conversation; we must choose between intoxication and cultivation of the mind. There are no drug-fiends among people who are primarily preoccupied with science and philosophy, art and literature.

CHAPTER 6

HOWEVER, let us concede the prohibitionist claims. Let us admit the police contention that cocaine and the rest are used by criminals who would otherwise lack the nerve to operate; they also contend that the effects of the drugs are so deadly that the cleverest thieves quickly become inefficient. Then for Heaven's sake establish depots where they can get free cocaine!

You cannot cure a drug fiend; you cannot make him a useful citizen. He never was a good citizen, or he would not have fallen into slavery. If you reform him temporarily, at vast expense, risk, and trouble, your whole work vanishes like morning mist when he meets his next temptation. The proper remedy is to let him *gang his ain gait to the de'il*. Instead of less drug, give him more drug, and be done with him.

His fate will be a warning to his neighbors, and in a year or two people will have the sense to shun the danger. Those who have not, let them die, too, and save the state. Moral weaklings are a danger to society, in whatever line their failings lie. If they are so amiable as to kill themselves, it is a crime to interfere.

You say that while these people are killing themselves they will do mischief. Maybe; but they are doing it now.

Prohibiton has created an underground traffic, as it always does; and the evils of this are immeasurable. Thousands of citizens are in league to defeat the law; are actually bribed by the law itself to do so, since the profits of the illicit trade become enormous, and the closer the prohibition, the more unreasonably big they are. You can stamp out the use of silk handkerchiefs in this way: people say, "All right; we'll use linen." But the "cocaine fiend" wants cocaine; and you can't put him off with Epsom salts. Moreover, his mind has lost all proportion; he will pay anything for his drug; he will never say, "I can't afford it"; and if the price be high, he will steal, rob, murder to get it. Again I say: you cannot reform a drug fiend; all you do by preventing them from obtaining it is to create a class of subtle and dangerous criminals; and even when you have jailed them all, is any one any the better?

While such large profits (from one thousand to two thousand per cent) are to be made by secret dealers, it is to the interest of these dealers to make new victims. And the profits at present are such that it would be worth my while to go to London and back first class to smuggle no more cocaine than I could hide in the lining of my overcoat! All expenses paid, and a handsome sum in the bank at the end of the trip! And for all the law, and the spies, and the rest of it, I could sell my stuff with very little risk in a single night in the Tenderloin.

Another point is this. Prohibition cannot be carried to its extreme. It is impossible, ultimately, to withhold drugs from doctors. Now doctors, more than any other single class, are drug fiends; and also, there are many who will traffic in drugs for the sake of money or power. If you possess a supply of the drug, you are the master, body and soul, of any person who needs it.

People do not understand that a drug, to its slave, is more valuable than gold or diamonds; a virtuous woman may be above rubies, but medical experience tells us that there is no virtuous woman in need of the drug who would not prostitute herself to a rag-picker for a single sniff.

And if it be really the case that one-fifth of the population takes some drug, then this long little, wrong little island is in for some very lively times.

The absurdity of the prohibitionist contention is shown by the experience of London and other European cities. In London any householder or apparently responsible person can buy any drug as easily as if it were cheese; and London is not full of raving maniacs, snuffing cocaine at every street corner, in the intervals of burglary, rape, arson, murder, malfeasance in office, and misprision of treason, as we are assured must be the case if a free people are kindly allowed to exercise a little freedom.

Or, if the prohibitionist contention be not absurd, it is a comment upon the moral level of the people of the United States which would have been righteously resented by the Gadarene swine after the devils had entered into them.

I am not here concerned to protest on their behalf; allowing the justice of the remark. I still say that prohibition is no cure. The cure is to give the people something to think about; to develop their minds; to fill them with ambitions beyond dollars; to set up a standard of achievement which is to be measured in terms of eternal realities; in a word, to educate them.

If this appear impossible, well and good; it is only another argument for encouraging them to take cocaine.

PART III

ABSINTHE: THE GREEN GODDESS

CHAPTER 1

KEEP always this dim corner for me, that I may sit while the Green Hour glides, a proud pavine of Time. For I am no longer in the city accursed, where Time is horsed on the white gelding Death, his spurs rusted with blood.

There is a corner of the United States which he has overlooked. It lies in New Orleans, between Canal Street and Esplanade Avenue; the Mississippi for its base. Thence it reaches northward to a most curious desert land, where is a cemetery lovely beyond dreams. Its walls low and whitewashed, within which straggles a wilderness of strange and fantastic tombs; and hard by is that great city of brothels which is so cynically mirthful a neighbor. As Felicien Rops wrote, — or was it Edmond d'Haraucourt? — *"la Prostitution et la Mort sont frere et soeur — les fils de Dieu!"* At least the poet of *Le Legende des Sexes* was right, and the psycho-analysts after him, in identifying the Mother with the Tomb.

This, then, is only the beginning and end of things, this *"quartier macabre"* beyond the North Rampart with the Mississippi on the other side. It is like the space between, our life which flows, and fertilizes as it flows, muddy and malarious as it may be, to empty itself into the warm bosom of the Gulf Stream, which (in our allegory) we may call the Life of God.

But our business is with the heart of things; we must go beyond the crude phenomena of nature if we are to dwell in the spirit. Art is the soul of life and the Old Absinthe House is heart and soul of the old quarter of New Orleans.

For here was the headquarters of no common man — no less than a real pirate — of Captain Lafitte, who not only robbed his neighbors, but defended them against invasion. Here, too, sat Henry Clay, who lived and died to give his name to a cigar. Outside this house no man remembers much more of him than that; but here, authentic and, as I imagine, indignant, his ghost stalks grimly.

Here, too are marble basins hollowed — and hallowed! — by the drippings of the water which creates by baptism the new spirit of absinthe.

I am only sipping the second glass of that "fascinating, but subtle poison, whose ravages eat men's heart and brain" that I have ever tasted in my life; and as I am not an American anxious for quick action, I am not surprised and disappointed that I do not drop dead upon the spot. But I can taste souls without the aid of absinthe; and besides, this is magic of absinthe! The spirit of the house has entered into it; it is an elixir, the masterpiece of an old alchemist, no common wine.

And so, as I talk with the patron concerning the vanity of things, I perceive the secret of the heart of God himself; this, that everything, even the vilest thing, is so unutterably lovely that it is worthy of the devotion of a God for all eternity.

What other excuse could He give man for making him? In substance, that is my answer to King Solomon.

CHAPTER 2

THE barrier between divine and human things is frail but inviolable; the artist and the *bourgeois* are only divided by a point of view — "A hair divided the false and true."

I am watching the opalescence of my absinthe, and it leads me to ponder upon a certain very curious mystery, persistent in legend. We may call it the mystery of the rainbow.

Originally in the fantastic but significant legend of the Hebrews, the rainbow is mentioned as the sign of salvation. The world has been purified by water, and was ready for the revelation of Wine. God would never again destroy His work, but ultimately seal its perfection by a baptism of fire.

Now, in this analogue also falls the coat of many colors which was made for Joseph, a legend which was regarded as so important that it was subsequently borrowed for the romance of Jesus. The veil of the Temple, too, was of many colors. We find, further east, that the *Manipura Cakkra* — the Lotus of the City of Jewels — which is an important centre in Hindu anatomy, and apparently identical with the solar plexus, is the central point of the nervous system of the human body, dividing the sacred from the profane, or the lower from the higher.

In western Mysticism, once more we learn that the middle grade initiation is called *Hodos Camelioniis,* the Path of the Chameleon. There is here evidently an allusion to this same mystery. We also learn that the middle stage in Alchemy is when the liquor becomes opalescent.

Finally, we note among the visions of the Saints one called the Universal Peacock, in which the totality is perceived thus royally appareled.

Would it were possible to assemble in this place the cohorts of quotation; for indeed they are beautiful with banners, flashing their myriad rays from cothurn and habergeon, gay and gallant in the light of that Sun which knows no fall from Zenith of high noon!

Yet I must needs already have written so much to make clear one pitiful conceit: can it be that in the opalescence of absinthe is some occult link with this mystery of the Rainbow? For undoubtedly one does indefinably and subtly insinuate the drinker in the secret chamber of Beauty, does kindle his thoughts to rapture, adjust his point of view to that of the artists, at least to that degree of which he is originally capable, weave for his fancy a gala dress of stuff as many-colored as the mind of Aphrodite.

Oh Beauty! Long did I love thee, long did I pursue thee, thee elusive, thee intangible! And lo! thou enfoldest me by night and day in the arms of gracious, of luxurious, of shimmering silence.

CHAPTER 3

THE Prohibitionist must always be a person of no moral character; for he cannot even conceive of the possibility of a man capable of resisting temptation. Still more, he is so obsessed, like the savage, by the fear of the unknown, that he regards alcohol as a fetish, necessarily alluring and tyrannical.

With this ignorance of human nature goes an ever grosser ignorance of the divine nature. He does not understand that the universe has only one possible purpose; that, the business of life being happily completed by the production of the necessities and luxuries incidental to comfort, the residuum of human energy needs an outlet. The surplus of Will must find issue in the elevation of the individual towards the Godhead; and the method of such elevation is by religion, love, and art. These three things are indissolubly bound up with wine, for they are species of intoxication.

Yet against all these things we find the prohibitionist, logically enough. It is true that he usually pretends to admit religion as a proper pursuit for humanity; but what a religion! He has removed from it every element of ecstasy or even of devotion; in his hands it has become cold, fanatical, cruel, and stupid, a thing merciless and formal, without sympathy or humanity. Love and art he rejects altogether; for him the only meaning of love is a mechanical — hardly even physiological! — process necessary for the perpetuation of the human race. (But why perpetuate it?) Art is for him the parasite and pimp of love. He cannot distinguish between the Apollo Belvedere and the crude bestialities of certain Pompeian frescoes, or between Rabelais and Elenor Glyn.

What then is his ideal of human life? one cannot say. So crass a creature can have no true ideal. There have been ascetic philosophers; but the prohibitionist would be as offended by their doctrine as by ours, which, indeed, are not so dissimilar as appears. Wage-slavery and boredom seem to complete his outlook on the world.

There are species which survive because of the feeling of disgust inspired by them: one is reluctant to set the heel firmly upon them, however thick may be one's boots. But when they are recognized as utterly noxious to humanity — the more so that they ape its form — then courage must be found, or, rather, nausea must be swallowed. May God send us a Saint George!

CHAPTER 4

IT is notorious that all genius is accompanied by vice. Almost always this takes the form of sexual extravagance. It is to be observed that deficiency, as in the cases of Carlyle and Ruskin, is to be reckoned as extravagance. At least the word abnormalcy will fit all cases. Farther, we see that in a very large number of great men there has also been indulgence in drink or drugs. There are whole periods when practically every great man has been thus marked, and these periods are those during which the heroic spirit has died out of their nation, and the *bourgeois* is apparently triumphant.

In this case the cause is evidently the horror of life induced in the artist by the contemplation of his surroundings. He must find another world, no matter at what cost.

Consider the end of the eighteenth century. In France the men of genius are made, so to speak, possible, by the Revolution. In England, under Castlereagh, we find Blake lost to humanity in mysticism, Shelley and Byron exiles, Coleridge taking refuge in opium, Keats sinking under the weight of circumstance, Wordsworth forced to sell his soul, while the enemy, in the persons of Southey and Moore, triumphantly holds sway.

The poetically similar period in France is 1850 to 1870. Hugo is in exile, and all his brethren are given to absinthe or to hashish or to opium.

There is however another consideration more important. There are some men who possess the understanding of the City of God, and know not the keys; or, if they possess them, have not force to turn them in the wards. Such men often seek to win heaven by forged credentials. Just so a youth who desires love is too often deceived by simulacra, embraces Lydia thinking her to be Lalage.

But the greatest men of all suffer neither the limitations of the former class nor the illusions of the latter. Yet we find them equally given to what is apparently indulgence. Lombroso has foolishly sought to find the source of this in madness — as if insanity could scale the peaks of Progress while Reason recoiled from the *bergschrund*. The explanation is far otherwise. Imagine to yourself the mental state of him who inherits or attains the full consciousness of the artist, that is to say, the divine consciousness.

He finds himself unutterably lonely, and he must steel himself to endure it. All his peers are dead long since! Even if he find an equal upon earth, there can scarcely be companionship, hardly more than the far courtesy of king to king. There are no twin souls in genius.

Good — he can reconcile himself to the scorn of the world. But yet he feels with anguish his duty towards it. It is therefore essential to him to be human.

Now the divine consciousness is not full flowered in youth. The newness of the objective world preoccupies the soul for many years. It is only as each illusion vanishes before the magic of the master that he gains more and more the power to dwell in the world of Reality. And with this comes the terrible temptation — the desire to enter and enjoy rather than remain among men and suffer their illusions. Yet, since the sole purpose of the incarnation of such a Master was to help humanity, they must make the supreme renunciation.

It is the problem of the dreadful bridge of Islam, *Al Sirak* — the razor-edge will cut the unwary foot, yet it must be trodden firmly, or the traveler will fall to the abyss. I dare not sit in the Old Absinthe House forever, wrapped in the ineffable delight of the Beatific Vision. I must write this essay, that men may thereby come at last to understand true things. But the operation of the creative godhead is not enough. Art is itself too near the reality which must be renounced for a season.

Therefore his work is also part of his temptation; the genius feels himself slipping constantly heavenward. The gravitation of eternity draws him. He is like a ship torn by the tempest from the harbor where the master must needs take on new passengers to the Happy Isles. So he must throw out anchors and the only holding is the mire! Thus in order to maintain the equilibrium of sanity, the artist is obliged to seek fellowship with the grossest of mankind. Like Lord Dunsany or Augustus John, today, or like Teniers of old, he may love to sit in taverns where sailors frequent; or he may wander the country with Gypsies, or he may form liaisons with the vilest men and women. Edward Fitzgerald would see an illiterate fisherman and spend weeks in his company. Verlaine made associates of Rimbaud and Bibi la Puree. Shakespeare consorted with the Earls of Pembroke and Southampton. Marlowe was actually killed during a brawl in a low tavern. And when we consider the sex-relation, it is hard to mention a genius who had a wife or mistress of even tolerable good character. If he had one, he would be sure to neglect her for a Vampire or a Shrew. A good woman is too near that heaven of Reality which he is sworn to renounce!

And this, I suppose, is why I am interested in the woman who has come to sit at the nearest table. Let us find out her story; let us try to see with the eyes of her soul!

CHAPTER 5

SHE is a woman of no more than thirty years of age, though she looks older. She comes here at irregular intervals, once a week or once a month, but when she comes she sits down to get solidly drunk on that alternation of beer and gin which the best authorities in England deem so efficacious.

As to her story, it is simplicity itself. She was kept in luxury for some years by a wealthy cotton broker, crossed to Europe with him, and lived in London and Paris like a Queen. Then she got the idea of "respectability" and "settling down in life"; so she married a man who could keep her in mere comfort. Result: repentance, and a periodical need to forget her sorrows. She is still "respectable"; she never tires of repeating that she is not one of "those girls" but "a married woman living far uptown," and that she "never runs about with men."

It is not the failure of marriage; it is the failure of men to recognize what marriage was ordained to be. By a singular paradox it is the triumph of the *bourgeois*. Only the hero is capable of marriage as the church understands it; for the marriage oath is a compact of appalling solemnity, an alliance of two souls against the world and against fate, with invocation of the great blessing of the Most High. Death is not the most beautiful of adventures, as Frohman said, for death is unavoidable; marriage is a voluntary heroism. That marriage has today become a matter of convenience is the last word of the commercial spirit. It is as if one should take a vow of knighthood to combat dragons — until the dragons appeared.

So this poor woman, because she did not understand that respectability is a lie, that it is love that makes marriage sacred and not the sanction of church or state, because she took marriage as an asylum instead of as a crusade, has failed in life, and now seeks alcohol under the same fatal error.

Wine is the ripe gladness which accompanies valor and rewards toil; it is the plume on a man's lancehead, a fluttering gallantry — not good to lean upon. Therefore her eyes are glassed with horror as she gazes uncomprehending upon her fate. That which she did all to avoid confronts her: she does not realize that, had she faced it, it would have fled with all the other phantoms. For the sole reality of this universe is God.

The Old Absinthe House is not a place. It is not bounded by four walls. It is headquarters to an army of philosophies. From this dim corner let me range, wafting thought through every air, salient against every problem of mankind: for it will always return like Noah's dove to this ark, this strange little sanctuary of the Green Goddess which has been set down not upon Ararat, but by the banks of the "Father of Waters."

CHAPTER 6

AH! the Green Goddess! What is the fascination that makes her so adorable and so terrible? Do you know that French sonnet *"La legende de l'absinthe?"* He must have loved it well, that poet. Here are his witnesses.

Apollon, qui pleurait le trepas d'Hyacinthe,
Ne voulait pas ceder la victoire a la mort.
Il fallait que son ame, adepte de l'essor,
Trouvat pour la beaute une alchemie plus sainte.
Donc de sa main celeste il epuise, il ereinte
Les dons les plus subtils de la divine Flore.
Leurs corps brises souspirent une exhalaison d'or
Dont il nous recueillait la goutte de — l'Absinthe!
Aux cavernes blotties, aux palis petillants,
Par un, par deux, buvez ce breuvage d'aimant!
Car c'est un sortilege, un propos de dictame,
Ce vin d'opale pale avortit la misere,
Ouvre de la beaute l'intime sanctuaire
—Ensorcelle mon coeur, extasie mort ame!

What is there in absinthe that makes it a separate cult? The effects of its abuse are totally distinct from those of other stimulants. Even in ruin and in degradation it remains a thing apart: its victims wear a ghastly aureole all their own, and in their peculiar hell yet gloat with a sinister perversion of pride that they are not as other men.

But we are not to reckon up the uses of a thing by contemplating the wreckage of its abuse. We do not curse the sea because of occasional disasters to our marines, or refuse axes to our woodsmen because we sympathize with Charles the First or Louis the Sixteenth. So therefore as special vices and dangers pertinent to absinthe, so also do graces and virtues that adorn no other liquor.

The word is from the Greek *apsinthion*. It means "undrinkable" or, according to some authorities, "undelightful." In either case, strange paradox! No: for the wormwood draught itself were bitter beyond human endurance; it must be aromatized and mellowed with other herbs.

Chief among these is the gracious Melissa, of which the great Paracelsus thought so highly that he incorporated it as the preparation of his *Ens Melissa Vitae*, which he expected to be an elixir of life and a cure for all diseases, but which in his hands never came to perfection.

Then also there are added mint, anise, fennel and hyssop, all holy herbs familiar to all from the Treasury of Hebrew Scripture. And there is even the sacred marjoram which renders man both chaste and passionate; the tender green angelica stalks also infused in this most mystic of concoctions; for like the *artemisia absinthium* itself it is a plant of Diana, and gives the purity and lucidity, with a touch of the madness, of the Moon; and above all there is the Dittany of Crete of which the eastern Sages say that one flower hath more puissance in high magic than all the other gifts of all the gardens of the world. It is as if the first diviner of absinthe had been indeed a magician intent upon a combination of sacred drugs which should cleanse, fortify and perfume the human soul.

And it is no doubt that in the due employment of this liquor such effects are easy to obtain. A single glass seems to render the breathing freer, the spirit lighter, the heart more ardent, soul and mind alike more capable of executing the great task of doing that particular work in the world which the Father may have sent them to perform. Food itself loses its gross qualities in the presence of absinthe and becomes even as *manna*, operating the sacrament of nutrition without bodily disturbance.

Let then the pilgrim enter reverently the shrine, and drink his absinthe as a stirrup-cup; for in the right conception of this life as an ordeal of chivalry lies the foundation of every perfection of philosophy. "Whatsoever ye do, whether ye eat or drink, do all to the glory of God!" applies with singular force to the *absintheur*. So may he come victorious from the battle of life to be received with tender kisses by some green-robed archangel, and crowned with mystic vervain in the Emerald Gateway of the Golden City of God.

CHAPTER 7

AND now the cafe is beginning to fill up. This little room with its dark green woodwork, its boarded ceiling, its sanded floor, its old pictures, its whole air of sympathy with time, is beginning to exert its magic spell. Here comes a curious child, short and sturdy, with a long blonde pigtail, with a jolly little old man who looks as if he had stepped straight out of the pages of Balzac.

Handsome and diminutive, with a fierce mustache almost as big as the rest of him, like a regular little Spanish fighting cock — Frank, the waiter, in his long white apron, struts to them with the glasses of ice-cold pleasure, green as the glaciers themselves. He will stand up bravely with the musicians bye and bye, and sing us a jolly song of old Catalonia.

The door swings open again. A tall dark girl, exquisitely slim and snaky, with masses of black hair knotted about her head, comes in. On her arm is a plump woman with hungry eyes, and a mass of Titian red hair. They seem distracted from the outer world, absorbed in some subject of enthralling interest and they drink their aperitif as if in a dream. I ask the mulatto boy who waits at my table (the sleek and lithe black panther!) who they are; but he knows only that one is a cabaret dancer, the other the owner of a cotton plantation up river. At a round table in the middle of the room sits one of the proprietors with a group of friends; he is burly, rubicund, and jolly, the very type of the Shakespearean "Mine host." Now a party of a dozen merry boys and girls comes in. The old pianist begins to play a dance, and in a moment the whole cafe is caught up in the music of harmonious motion. Yet still the invisible line is drawn about each soul; the dance does not conflict with the absorption of the two strange women, or with my own mood of detachment.

Then there is a "little laughing lewd gamine" dressed all in black save for a square white collar. Her smile is broad and free as the sun and her gaze as clean and wholesome and inspiring. There is the big jolly blonde Irish girl in the black velvet beret and coat, and the white boots, chatting with two boys in khaki from the border. There is the Creole girl in pure white cap-a-pie, with her small piquant face and its round button of a nose, and its curious deep rose flush, and its red little mouth, impudently smiling. Around these islands seems to flow as a general tide the more stable life of the quarter. Here are honest good-wives seriously discussing their affairs, and heaven only knows if it be love or the price of sugar which engages them so wholly. There are but a few commonplace and uninteresting elements in the cafe; and these are without exception men. The giant Big Business is a great tyrant! He seizes all the men for slaves, and leaves the women to make shift as best they can for — all that makes life worth living. Candies and American Beauty Roses are of no use in an emergency. So, even in this most favored corner, there is dearth of the kind of men that women need.

At the table next to me sits an old, old man. He has done great things in his day, they tell me, an engineer, who first found it possible to dig Artesian wells in the Sahara desert. The Legion of Honor glows red in his shabby surtout. He comes here, one of the many wrecks of the Panama Canal, a piece of jetsam cast up by that tidal wave of speculation and corruption. He is of the old type, the thrifty peasantry; and he has his little income from the Rente. He says that he is too old to cross the ocean — and why should he, with the atmosphere of old France to be had a stone's throw from his little apartment in Bourbon Street? It is a curious type of house that one finds in this quarter in New Orleans; meagre without, but within one comes unexpectedly upon great spaces, carved wooden balconies on which the rooms open. So he dreams away his honored days in the Old Absinthe House. His rusty black, with its worn red button, is a noble wear.

Black, by the way, seems almost universal among the women: is it instinctive good taste? At least, it serves to bring up the general level of good looks. Most American women spoil what little beauty they may have by overdressing. Here there is nothing extravagant, nothing vulgar, none of the near-Paris-gown and the lust-off-Bond-Street hat. Nor is there a single dress to which a Quaker could object. There is neither the mediocrity nor the immodesty of the New York woman, who is tailored or millinered on a garish pattern, with the Eternal Chorus Girl as the Ideal — an ideal which she always attains, though (Heaven knows!) in "society" there are few "front row" types.

On the other side of me a splendid stalwart maid, modern in muscle, old only in the subtle and modest fascination of her manner, her face proud, cruel and amorous, shakes her wild tresses of gold in pagan laughter. Her mood is universal as the wind. What can her cavalier be doing to keep her waiting? It is a little mystery which I will not solve for the reader; on the contrary—

CHAPTER 8

YES, it was my own sweetheart (no! not all the magazines can vul-
garize that loveliest of words) who was waiting for me to be done with
my musings. She comes in silently and stealthily, preening and purr-
ing like a great cat, and sits down, and begins to Enjoy. She knows I
must never be disturbed until I close my pen. We shall go together to
dine at a little Italian restaurant kept by an old navy man, who
makes the best ravioli this side of Genoa; then we shall walk the wet
and windy streets, rejoicing to feel the warm sub-tropical rain upon
our faces. We shall go down to the Mississippi, and watch the lights of
the ships, and listen to the tales of travel and adventure of the mari-
ners. There is one tale that moves me greatly; it is like the story of
the sentinel of *Herculaneum*. A cruiser of the U.S. Navy was detailed
to Rio de Janeiro. (This was before the days of wireless telegraphy.)
The port was in quarantine; the ship had to stand ten miles out to
sea.

Nevertheless, Yellow Jack managed to come aboard. The men died
one by one. There was no way of getting word to Washington; and, as
it turned out later, the Navy Department had completely forgotten
the existence of the ship. No orders came; the captain stuck to his
post for three months. Three months of solitude and death! At last a
passing ship was signaled, and the cruiser was moved to happier waters. No doubt the story is a lie; but did that make it less splendid in
the telling, as the old scoundrel sat and spat and chewed tobacco? No,
we will certainly go down, and ruffle it on the wharves. There is really
better fun in life than going to the movies, when you know how to
sense Reality.

There is beauty in every incident of life; the true and the false, the
wise and the foolish, are all one in the eye that beholds all without
passion or prejudice: and the secret appears to lie not in the retire-
ment from the world, but in keeping a part of oneself Vestal, sacred,
intact, aloof from that self which makes contact with the external
universe. In other words, in a separation of that which is and perceives from that which acts and suffers. And the art of doing this is
really the art of being an artist. As a rule, it is a birthright; it may

perhaps be attained by prayer and fasting; most surely, it can never be bought.

But if you have it not, this will be the best way to get it — or something like it. Give up your life completely to the task; sit daily for six hours in the Old Absinthe House, and sip the icy opal; endure till all things change insensibly before your eyes, you changing with them; till you become as gods, knowing good and evil, and that they are not two but one.

It may be a long time before the veil lifts; but a moment's experience of the point of view of the artist is worth a myriad martyrdoms. It solves every problem of life and death — which two also are one.

It translates this universe into intelligible terms, relating truly the ego with the non-ego, and recasting the prose of reason in the poetry of soul. Even as the eye of the sculptor beholds his masterpiece already existing in the shapeless mass of marble, needing only the loving kindness of the chisel to cut away the veils of Isis, so you may (perhaps) learn to behold the sum and summit of all grace and glory from this great observatory, the Old Absinthe House of New Orleans.

V'la, p'tite chatte; c'est fini, le travail. Foutons le camp!

ABOUT THE AUTHOR

ALEISTER CROWLEY, born Edward Alexander Crowley; 12 October 1875 – 1 December 1947, was an English occultist, ceremonial magician, poet, painter, novelist, and mountaineer. He was the founder of Thelema, identifying himself as the prophet entrusted with guiding humanity into the Æon of Horus in the early 20th century. A prolific writer, he published widely over the course of his life.

Born to a wealthy Plymouth Brethren family in Royal Leamington Spa, Warwickshire, Crowley rejected his fundamentalist Christian faith to pursue an interest in Western esotericism. He was educated at the University of Cambridge, where some biographers allege he was recruited into the British intelligence agency. In 1898 he joined the esoteric Hermetic Order of the Golden Dawn and was trained in ceremonial magic by Samuel Liddell MacGregor Mathers and Allan Bennett. After moving to Boleskine House by Loch Ness in Scotland, he went mountaineering in Mexico with Oscar Eckenstein, before studying Hindu and Buddhist practices in India. He married Rose Edith Kelly, and in 1904 they honey-mooned in Cairo, Egypt, where Crowley claimed to have been contacted by a supernatural entity named Aiwass, who provided him with The Book of the Law, a sacred text that served as the basis for Thelema. Announcing the start of the Æon of Horus, The Book declared that its followers should adhere to the code of "Do what thou wilt" and seek to align themselves with their Will through the practice of magick.

After an unsuccessful attempt to climb Kanchenjunga and a visit to India and China, Crowley returned to Britain, where he attracted attention as a prolific author of poetry, novels, and occult literature. In 1907, he and George Cecil Jones co-founded a Thelemite order, the A∴A∴, through which they propagated their religion. After spending time in Algeria, in 1912 he was initiated into another esoteric order, the German-based Ordo Templi Orientis (O.T.O.), rising to become the leader of its British branch, which he reformulated in accordance with his Thelemite beliefs. Through the O.T.O., Thelemite groups were established in Britain, Australia, and North America.

Crowley spent the First World War in the United States, where he took up painting and campaigned for the German war effort against Britain, later revealing that he had infiltrated the pro-German movement to assist the British intelligence services. In 1920, he established the Abbey of Thelema, a religious commune in Cefalù, Sicily where he lived with various followers. His libertine lifestyle led to denunciations in the British press, and expulsion by the Mussolini in 1923. He divided the following two decades between France, Germny, and England, and continued to promote Thelema until his death in 1947.

Crowley gained widespread notoriety during his lifetime, being a recreational drug experimenter, bisexual and an individualist social critic. He was denounced in the popular press as "the wickedest man in the world" and a Satanist. Crowley has remained a highly influential figure over Western esotericism and the counter-culture, and continues to be considered a prophet in Thelema.

ABOUT THE EDITOR

ELIZABETH LEDBETTER is a researcher and writer focusing on the history, philosophy and structure of alternative religions. Her interest in this area stems from her traditional Catholic upbringing, which exposed her to the colorful world of angels and saints—along with their more hellish counterparts. After lapsing from the Church, her spiritual nature asserted itself and led her on a search for a replacement to the religion she left behind. Her journey has been fulfilling; she has encountered and studied a number of diverse faiths and beliefs from the New Age and Occult communities. She has had the pleasure of meeting and learning from the independent and intriguing people who find themselves on the outside of mainstream religion. She enjoys searching out ancient or forgotten texts for her studies and bringing them to new audiences in modern formats. She holds a history degree from a large public university in the South and lives in Tennessee with her husband and two dogs.